WELCOME
TO THE FAMILY

WELCOME
TO THE FAMILY
WHAT TO EXPECT NOW
THAT YOU'RE A CHRISTIAN

JOHN MACARTHUR

THOMAS NELSON
Since 1798

NASHVILLE   DALLAS   MEXICO CITY   RIO DE JANEIRO

Published in Nashville, Tennessee, by Thomas Nelson. Thomas Nelson is a registered trademark of Thomas Nelson, Inc.

Nelson Books titles may be purchased in bulk for educational, business, fund-raising, or sales promotional use. For information, please e-mail SpecialMarkets@ThomasNelson.com.

Published in association with the literary agency of Wolgemuth & Associates, Inc.

Unless otherwise noted, Scripture quotations are from THE NEW KING JAMES VERSION. Copyright © 1979, 1980, 1982 by Thomas Nelson, Inc., Publishers. Used by permission. All rights reserved.

Scripture quotations noted NASB the are from NEW AMERICAN STANDARD BIBLE®, © Copyright The Lockman Foundation 1960, 1962, 1963, 1968, 1971, 1972, 1973, 1975, 1977, 1995. Used by permission. *www.Lockman.org*

Library of Congress Cataloging-in-Publication Data

MacArthur, John, 1939–
    Welcome to the family : what to expect now that you're a Christian / John MacArthur.
      p. cm.
  ISBN 0-7852-8042-1 (tp)
  ISBN 0-7852-6348-9 (hc)
  1. Christian life. I. Title.
  BV4501.3.M215 2004
  248.4—dc22

2004010429

Printed in the United States of America
05 06 07 08 09 QG 9 8 7 6 5 4 3 2 1

CONTENTS

INTRODUCTION

THE NEW YOU

*S*uddenly everything is different.

The old you is gone forever, and a new you has taken its place. You're a Christian now, and I thank God for saving you and making you His own. Whatever process or experience brought you to this point, it is the most wonderful and important transformation of your life. It is a watershed event, not only because of the deep sense of joy and satisfaction that comes with knowing you belong to the family of God, but because as a Christian you are absolutely assured of eternal life in heaven. The blessings of God through Jesus Christ are yours *forever*.

Your faith journey may have been relatively easy or very hard. However you traveled, however you suffered along the way, you now have a Companion and Guide who will never leave you. This is an exhilarating time; it can also be scary and confusing. You may have already discovered that being a Christian will cost you friends and old pastimes.

It may cost you more than that. Jesus made the conditions clear in Luke 9:23, when He said, "If anyone desires to come after Me, let him deny himself, and take up his cross daily, and follow Me." As a Christian you have to be willing to give up anything Jesus asks you to, even if it's everything. Even if it's your life. True love for God means total disdain and denial of *you*. To deny yourself, to come to the understanding that you're a worthless sinner in need of God's gift of salvation, is the biggest hurdle you'll ever face. You left behind a lot in that other world—at least that is what the world would have you believe. But what you have gained far outweighs anything and everything you once possessed.

You'll also learn that what would have seemed like a great sacrifice before is little or no sacrifice when done to follow Christ. Giving up something because He wants it is such an honor that you might not miss it at all. I played football in college, and when I graduated, three NFL teams asked me if I'd like to play in the pros. I thought about it, but decided to go into the ministry instead. It wasn't a sacrifice; it was answering God's call. And I've never regretted it.

Becoming a Christian is like being adopted into a new family. The Apostle Paul used this comparison in his letter to the Romans: "For as many as are led by the Spirit of God, these are sons of God. For you did not receive the spirit of bondage again to fear, but you have received the Spirit of adoption by whom we cry out, 'Abba, Father.' The Spirit Himself bears witness with our spirit that we are children of God" (8:14–16). As Christians, we have been adopted by God into His family and receive His intimate, fatherly love, grace, and compassion.

Just as a husband and wife show love and compassion to a parentless child by making him a member of their family, God grants us grace by bringing us into His family and giving us all the same rights and privileges His other children have. In the Roman culture of Paul's day, an adopted child, especially a son, usually received greater prestige and privilege than the natural children of a family, particularly if the father was disappointed in his own children. That's what happens as a result of your spiritual adoption by God. He graciously and lovingly sought you out and made you His child, solely on the basis of your trust in His eternal Son, Jesus Christ. Because of your adoption, you will share in the full inheritance of Christ Himself.

You became His child the instant you were saved: "But as many as received Him, to them He gave the right to become children of God, to those who believe in His name" (John 1:12). You can now address God in an intimate way, as "Abba," the Aramaic term for "Daddy."

Simply put, your adoption means that the life of God dwells intimately in you. He is your "Daddy" in a way no human parent can be. Human parents can adopt children and love them as much as they do their natural children, but they can't impart their nature to an adopted child. Yet that is exactly what God has done for you. You have become a partaker "of the divine nature" (2 Peter 1:4) in that the Spirit of God dwells in you.

You and I became God's children, not through our own ability or effort, but because He sovereignly chose us "before the foundation of the world, that we should be holy and without blame before Him in love, having predestined us to adoption as sons by Jesus Christ to Himself"(Ephesians 1:4–5). He has made you His child in the image of His Son, giving you not just Christ's riches and blessings, but also His very nature.

As beautiful and rich in meaning as the adoption metaphor is, it falls short in explaining all that happened to you when God saved you. Like adoptive human parents, God strikes a balance between unconditional love and chastening correction. But He is your Creator as well as your Father. He knows you in a way no earthly father ever could. And He loves you with superhuman love; in fact, He sent His perfect Son to die for your sins. He saved you from spiritual death, and as a result you were spiritually reborn, justified, and now are being sanctified. One day you will be glorified.

Why did God save you? Paul says it was "according to the good pleasure of his will, to the praise of the glory of His grace" (Ephesians 1:5–6). Above all else, God chose to save you for His own glory. As your spiritual journey continues, you'll see yourself reflecting more and more of that glory in your life. Second Corinthians 3:18 says, "But we all, with unveiled face, beholding as in a mirror the glory of the Lord, are being transformed into the same image from glory to glory, just as by the Spirit of the Lord." It is my prayer that this book will help you along that ever-transforming path.

ONE LOVE

Before you were saved, mostly you loved only one person—yourself. Paul shows his understanding of this natural self-centeredness in Ephesians 2: "We all once conducted ourselves in the lusts of our flesh, fulfilling the desires of the flesh and of the mind, and were by nature children of wrath, just as the others. But God, who is rich in mercy, because of His great love with which He loved us, even when we were dead in trespasses, made us alive together with Christ" (verses 3–5).

You were dead! You may have been alive physically, but you were dead spiritually. Now you have a new life in Christ. God has made you alive to the spiritual realm and transformed you with a new capacity to love. Your one love above all others is for God, which is completely different from the kind of love the world understands and admires.

Luke 10 recounts a discussion between Jesus and a lawyer who wants to know what he has to do to inherit eternal life.

When Jesus asks the lawyer what he thinks is written in the law, the lawyer answers, "You shall love the LORD your God with all your heart, with all your soul, with all your strength, and with all your mind," and that you should love "your neighbor as yourself." Jesus answered, "You have answered rightly; do this and you will live" (verses 25–28; also Matthew 22:34–40).

The command to love God with all one's heart, soul, and mind was part of what Jewish people call the Shema, which contained the texts of Deuteronomy 6:4–9; 11:13–21; and Numbers 15:37–41. They were the most familiar and most quoted Scripture passages in Judaism, sometimes written and placed in boxes strapped on the arm and on a home's doorpost. Even in Jesus' day faithful Jews would recite the Shema twice a day.

The lawyer easily got the right answer. The way to eternal life is to love God with *all* our hearts, souls, strength, and minds. *Agape* love, the Greek equivalent to the Hebrew *aheb*, is the love of the mind, will, emotion, and affection. It is the love Jesus describes, the highest kind of love.

The implication here is that to obey the greatest commandment—and to inherit eternal life as a result—Christians must love God perfectly with their *entire* beings. That is an impossible goal for sinful humankind. The lawyer knew he didn't love God like that. The religious leaders knew they couldn't either. And neither can you and I. So our eternal life comes only by God's grace.

THE MARK OF SALVATION

But to love God as fully as humanly possible, you have to deny yourself, take up your cross daily, and follow Jesus wherever He leads, as we saw in Luke 9:23. How can you love God when you're in the way? You can't. Salvation is not about self-fulfillment; it's about self-denial. It's not about self-love; it's about self-hate. When pride dominates the sinner's life, there's certainly no room to love God, let alone love Him perfectly.

That was Paul's point when he said, "By the deeds of the law no flesh will be justified in His sight, for by the law is the knowledge of sin" (Romans 3:20). It is impossible for wretched sinners like you and me to love God as we should.

At one time in his life, Paul thought he was doing all he could to prove his love for God. By the standards of works-righteousness religion, his credentials were absolutely stellar. He was "circumcised the eighth day, of the stock of Israel, of the tribe of Benjamin, a Hebrew of the Hebrews; concerning the law, a Pharisee; concerning zeal, persecuting the church; concerning the righteousness which is in the law, blameless" (Philippians 3:5–6). According to the conventional religious wisdom of his day, Paul followed the right rituals, was a member of the right race and tribe, adhered to the right traditions, served the right religion with more than the right amount of intensity, and conformed to the right law with self-righteous zeal.

But one day while traveling to persecute more Christians, Paul met Jesus Christ (Acts 9). He saw Christ in all His majesty and realized that all he considered valuable was worthless, and the One he thought he loved, he hated. "But what things were gain to me, these I have counted loss for Christ," he cried. "Yet indeed I also count all things loss . . . and count them as rubbish, that I may gain Christ" (Philippians 3:7–8). That is the essence of self-denial. In Paul's mind, his assets had become liabilities—nothing but trash. Why? Because they couldn't produce the righteousness and salvation he once thought they could. So they couldn't lead him to eternal life. He said, "For I know that in me (that is, in my flesh) nothing good dwells" (Romans 7:18). So he gave up all his earthly religious treasure for the heavenly riches of knowing Christ deeply and intimately.

Paul's example shows us that the distinguishing mark of saving belief in God is loving God. Faith in Jesus Christ that is not characterized by love for Him is not saving faith. The new creation that takes place at salvation produces a new will, desire, and attitude deep within you, an *agape* love for God that radiates out from the very core of your being. That love means a desire to please and honor Him above all others.

The apostle John also made love for God the true mark of the believer. He quoted Jesus, saying, "If anyone loves Me, he will keep My word; and My Father will love him, and We will come to him and make Our home with him. He who does not love Me does not keep My words; and the word which you hear is not Mine but the Father's who sent Me" (John 14:23–24). In his first epistle, John wrote, "But whoever keeps His word, truly the love of God is perfected in him. By this we know that we are in Him" (1 John 2:5; see also 3:17; 4:12–13). You'll notice how these verses connect love for God with keeping His Word.

Where does this ability to love come from? John explained, "He who does not love does not know God, for God is love" (1 John 4:8). The source of our love is its very object, the One who is the essence of love, whether expressed in consolation or in wrath and judgment.

Jesus enabled us to receive His love because He died for our sin of hating God. Now He enables us to love God, because it is through Him that "the love of God has been poured out in our hearts by the Holy Spirit who was given to us" (Romans 5:5). First John 4:19 confirms this wonderful truth: "We love Him because He first loved us."

THE SOURCE OF JOY

As a result of your salvation, a love for the Lord Jesus Christ is the driving priority of your life. Peter summed up this priority when, speaking of Christ, he said, "Whom having not seen you love. Though now you do not see Him, yet believing, you rejoice with joy inexpressible and full of glory" (1 Peter 1:8).

It is normal to love someone you know well. But Peter was writing to Christians who, like us, had never met Jesus face-to-face. They had never touched Him, walked with Him, shared a meal with Him, heard His voice, felt His hands, or gazed into His eyes. Yet they loved and trusted Him, which resulted in inexpressible joy. As a Christian, loving Christ becomes the great passion of your life even though you can never meet Him this side of heaven.

Peter understood this principle from personal experience. Except for Judas Iscariot, who betrayed Jesus, Peter demonstrated the least degree of trust of any disciple, denying Christ on three occasions (Matthew 26:69–75). And Jesus repeatedly questioned the validity of his love, once specifically asking him, "O you of little faith, why did you doubt?" (Matthew 14:31).

I feel sure that as Peter implored readers to love and trust Christ, whom they had never seen, he was mindful of his failure to do the same thing after spending three years in His presence! Peter failed, yet the Lord graciously forgave him and restored him to ministry. Peter learned to love and trust Christ deeply. In the same way, God's Spirit patiently teaches us to love and trust the Lord.

In 1 Corinthians 13:7, Paul says that love "believes all things." We see how love and trust are inextricably linked in the cycle of Christian growth: God grants you faith, and by faith you grasp the biblical teachings about Jesus Christ. As your knowledge of Him increases, your love and trust grow deeper and stronger. Increasingly you desire to glorify Him by serving Him wholeheartedly, talking and reading about Him, communing with Him, thus getting to know Him better and becoming increasingly like Him.

Seventeenth-century Anglican archbishop Robert Leighton wrote:

Believe, and you shall love; believe much, and you shall love much; labor for strong and deep persuasions of the glorious things which are spoken of Christ, and this will command love. Certainly, did men indeed believe his worth, they would accordingly love him; for the reasonable creature cannot but affect that most which it firmly believes to be the worthiest of affection. Oh! this mischievous unbelief is that which makes the heart cold and dead toward God. Seek then to believe Christ's excellency in himself, and his love to us, and our interest in him, and this will kindle such a fire in the heart, as will make it ascend in a sacrifice of love to Him. (*Commentary on First Peter* [Grand Rapids: Kregel, 1972 reprint], 55)

Leighton's words reaffirm that love and trust are at the heart of our relationship to Christ and the joy it brings. Peter referred to "joy inexpressible and full of glory" (1 Peter 1:8). The Greek word for "inexpressible" contains the sense of a divine mystery exceeding the powers of speech and thought. Even on a human level it is difficult to communicate the joy of loving others—look at the countless thousands of love songs that have made the attempt. But beyond that level is the inexpressible joy that comes from loving Christ. It is a heavenly joy, full of glory, because our love is a heavenly love.

THE HEART OF CHRISTIANITY

It's no wonder that Paul expressed his love for Christ so profoundly:

I also count all things loss for the excellence of the knowledge of Christ Jesus my Lord, for whom I have suffered the loss of all things, and count them as rubbish, that I may gain Christ and be found in Him, not having my own righteousness, which is from the law, but that which is through faith in Christ, the righteousness which is from God by faith; that I may know Him and the power of His resurrection, and the fellowship of His sufferings, being conformed to His death, if, by any means, I may attain to the resurrection from the dead. (Philippians 3:8–11)

The heart and soul of the Christian life is our love for Christ. Our salvation begins with Him, our sanctification progresses with Him, and our glorification ends with Him. He is the reason for our being, and thus He is more precious to us than anyone or anything.

Paul knew well that the heart of the Christian life is building an intimate knowledge of Christ when he said, "I count all things to be loss in view of the surpassing value of knowing Christ Jesus my Lord" (Philippians 3:8 NASB). That was both his passion and his goal (verse 14).

The essence of salvation is an exchange of something worthless for something valuable. That's what happens to those whom God chooses to bring into His kingdom. The person who comes to God is willing to give up whatever He requires, no matter how high the price. When confronted with his sin in the light of the glory of Christ—when God takes the blinders off his eyes—the repentant sinner suddenly realizes that nothing he held dear is worth keeping if it means losing Christ.

At some point in your life, you discovered that Jesus Christ was far more valuable than anything you had. All possessions, fame, and desires became worthless compared to Christ. So you trashed them all and turned to Him as your Savior and Lord. He became the supreme object of your affections. Your new desire is to know Him, honor Him, serve Him, obey Him, and be like Him. Those are the fruits of your new relationship with Jesus Christ, Lord of the universe, which result in righteousness, power, fellowship, and glory.

The One you are commanded to love is worthy of that love. God has given you a new life centered on Christ that changes everything else.

2

ACTIONS SPEAK LOUDEST

*H*ow can you show God the overwhelming love you hold for Him in your heart? You show it by doing what He wants you to do. We say that actions speak louder than words. When it comes to proving our love for God, actions speak louder than any promise or proclamation we can make. The best way to prove your love and demonstrate your honor for Christ is to obey Him and submit to Him in everything.

As a new member of God's family, you now have within you the desire and ability to do what pleases Him. And that is also how you display your love to Him. Love and obedience are inseparable.

The Bible is filled from beginning to end with examples of the importance of obedience to the will of God, and the reminder that what a person does reveals the true feelings of his heart. There was never a time or place in the Old

Testament when God commanded external obedience apart from internal motivation. In Exodus 20:6, God shows "mercy to thousands, to those who love [Him] and keep [His] commandments." Obedience was always commanded from willing hearts.

In the New Testament, Jesus declared, "If you love Me, keep My commandments . . . He who has My commandments and keeps them, it is he who loves Me" (John 14:15, 21). The apostle John wrote, "Now by this we know that we know Him, if we keep His commandments . . . Whoever keeps His word, truly the love of God is perfected in him" (1 John 2:3, 5). If you belong to God—if you are indeed an adopted member of His family—you will love and obey Him.

The obedience of a true believer will be unequivocal, uncompromising, sincere, and an integral part of his salvation. In fact, the apostle Peter actually described salvation as an act of obedience: "Since you have purified your souls in obeying the truth through the Spirit in sincere love of the brethren . . . having been born again, not of corruptible seed but incorruptible, through the word of God which lives and abides forever" (1 Peter 1:22–23). The "truth" is the gospel, which is essentially a command to repent and believe in the Lord Jesus Christ. In the New Testament, the gospel message was always preached as a command (Matthew 3:2; 4:17; Mark 6:12; Luke 5:32; Acts 2:38; 3:19; 17:30; 26:20). As a command it calls for obedience. Anyone who is genuinely born again has a new spiritual life because he heard the truth of Scripture, believed it, and obeyed it.

However, the moment of salvation involves more than an isolated act of obedience. In the beginning, obedience to God can be frustrating at best and seemingly overwhelming at worst. Like an adopted son or daughter, you won't understand the commands or be able to obey them all at once. The same way an adopted child has to learn gradually what to do in the family, you must learn gradually what to do in this new Christian context. The reality of your commitment to Christ doesn't hit you all at once. It unfolds over time like a flower. As God's will in Scripture becomes clearer, you become more obedient and more eager to improve even further.

The reason we don't immediately understand all the ramifications of our commitment to Christ is that God, through the Holy Spirit, must first give us that sense of dedication. Commitment does not originate with us. The Spirit produces in our hearts the willingness to travel the pathway of obedience to God as servants of Jesus Christ.

When you came to a saving faith in Him, you entered

a whole new realm of obedience. Up to then you obeyed the flesh, the world, and the devil and were controlled by all the various facets of sin (see 1 John 2:15–16). But as a believer, you are eager to be obedient to the righteousness of Christ.

WHY WE OBEY

First John 2:3 says, "Now by this we know that we know Him, if we keep His commandments." The word *keep* here carries the idea of watchful obedience. It's not obedience externally motivated by force or pressure, but internal obedience out of pure love for the Master.

The Greek word translated "keep" means "to watch or guard as some precious thing." A Christian demonstrates he knows God by a heartfelt desire to guard his obedience as a treasure. People who claim to be Christians, yet live in disregard for God's commandments, undermine their testimony and call into question the validity of their claim to know Christ.

The word that John uses for "commandments," *entole*, is also significant. In 1 John the apostle uses it to refer to the precepts of Christ at least fourteen times. If you exhibit a recurring spirit of obedience toward safeguarding the precepts of Christ, a regular desire that they be honored, and a consistent determination to obey them, then you have come to know God and the Lord Jesus Christ. When you sincerely enthrone Christ, you gladly submit to His authority.

To an outsider—and to many new Christians if we're honest with ourselves—obedience to the will of God can seem incredibly hard and unpleasant, if not impossible. Deny yourself? Take up a cross? You can't be serious! But in 1 John 5:2–3 the apostle reminds us of a startling and reassuring truth: "By this we know that we love the children of God, when we love God and keep His commandments. For this is the love of God, that we keep His commandments. And His commandments are not burdensome." As Jesus Himself said, "My yoke is easy and My burden is light" (Matthew 11:30).

There's a chain of events that takes place in the hearts of Christians: We believe in God; we have faith in Christ, who is God; our faith produces love; that love produces obedience. If you believe Christ is who He claims to be, then He will draw all the love, praise, and adoration out of your heart, and you will be consumed with Him. And those who truly love Him in that way express their love by keeping His commandments, bearing His easy yoke with joy.

Paul offered some clarification on why obedience to God's commands is not a burden:

Do you not know that to whom you present yourselves slaves to obey, you are that one's slaves whom you obey, whether of sin leading to death, or of obedience leading to righteousness? But God be thanked that though you were slaves of sin, yet you obeyed from the heart that form of doctrine to which you were delivered. And having been set free from sin, you became slaves of righteousness. (Romans 6:16–18)

A slave's primary duty is obedience—to do whatever the master tells him to do. That is true in the spiritual realm, whether someone is an unbeliever and a slave to sin, or a believer and a slave to Christ. But Paul then applied that simple illustration to the crucial phrase "obeyed from the heart." Heart obedience ought to be the overriding attitude and desire in your life. You should obey because you *want* to, not because anyone is forcing you to. It means obedience is a fundamental, inner trait of your new life, and you become so singularly obedient to God's Word that you are called a slave of righteousness.

You delight to obey God's law because you love Him. Yes, loving is a duty—it is an act of the will—but it is not oppressive. Why is it so delightful to obey Him? Because God's law is a reflection of Himself and the way we love Him. Obedience to His law pleases both Him and Christians who love Him and seek His pleasure.

LAW VERSUS GRACE

Still, the harsh reality is that every Christian fails to follow Christ perfectly, because every Christian has a sinful nature. Yet there's an important distinction between legal obedience and gracious obedience.

Legal obedience is the result of fleshly effort. It demands an absolute, perfect obedience without a single failure. It says that if you violate God's law even once, the penalty is death.

Gracious obedience is a loving and sincere spirit of submission motivated by God's grace to us. Though often defective, this obedience is nevertheless accepted by God, for its blemishes are blotted out by the blood of Jesus Christ.

What a difference! With fleshly, human effort, obedience must be perfect to be of any value. With divine grace, God looks at the heart, not the works. If God measured my legal obedience against His standard, I would spend eternity in hell. But God looks at me and sees a heart redeemed by Christ that longs to obey Him and a spirit that wills to submit to His lordship, even though that willingness is far from perfect.

Do you remember when Peter was frustrated in convincing the Lord that he, though disobedient, loved Him? What did Peter finally say to get the Lord to accept his confession of love? He didn't say, "Look at my obedience," since he was caught disobeying. He said, "Lord, You know all things; You know that I love You" (John 21:17).

That is the point of the cross of Christ. Jesus died, bearing the full penalty for our sins and failings, so that His blood can cover whatever is defective in our day-to-day love and obedience.

Certainly even the apostles didn't always obey God. All of them failed the Lord and made mistakes because they, too, were sinful. Yet concerning them, Jesus could tell the Father, "They have kept Your word" (John 17:6). Did they keep it perfectly? Of course not. Their desire and determination to submit to Jesus Christ were what Jesus measured, not a legalistic, absolute standard.

God's standard of holiness is still absolute perfection, but He has graciously made provision for our inevitable failures. If we do something wrong, He doesn't say we are no longer Christians. He looks with favor on those who have a spirit of obedience. The true Christian has a desire to submit to Jesus Christ, even though he can't always fulfill that desire. But God discerns and graciously accepts it.

God knows what's inside because He has written His law in your heart: "I will put My law in their minds, and write it on their hearts; and I will be their God, and they shall be My people" (Jeremiah 31:33). Psalm 40:8 says, "I delight to do Your will, O my God, and Your law is within my heart."

Scripture confirms that whatever is in a man's heart controls how he lives: "For as he thinks in his heart, so is he" (Proverbs 23:7). Those who truly know God—those who love Him—will be moved in their hearts to obey the law God wrote there.

THE PERFECT PATTERN

Though we can't obey God perfectly, we can and do try to pattern our lives after the one Person in history who could obey with perfection—Jesus Christ. He shows you by example what to do if you will only follow Him.

First John 2:6 tells us, "He who says he abides in Him ought himself also to walk just as He walked." John used the word *abides* to mean "knowing Him," "walking in the light," and "being in fellowship." All those terms indicate salvation. The point is that if you declare yourself to be a Christian, you ought to show a pattern of walking in the same manner as He walked. That doesn't mean your life will be exactly like His, but you will walk with a desire to please God as He did. Christ is our pattern—we ought to live as He lived as nearly as possible. Loving obedience moves us toward Christlikeness.

Philippians 2:8 says of Jesus: "Being found in appearance as a man, He humbled Himself and became obedient to the point of death, even the death of the cross." Jesus was in the form of God, but He did not insist on hanging on to that glory and privilege. Instead, He was willing to temporarily set them aside and humble Himself. That is the greatest illustration of humility ever. Jesus said, "I have come down from heaven, not to do My own will, but the will of Him who sent Me" (John 6:38). His entire attitude was marked by a spirit of obedience. And that is the pattern of loving obedience we are to imitate. Obedience to Christ and His Word is the ultimate proof of the reality of your love for Him. What you say about your love for Him is relatively unimportant—what counts is that you show your love for Him by how you live your life.

The Bible is filled with examples of ways you can demonstrate your love for God. Here are a few:

- Meditate on God's glory (Psalm 18:1–3).

- Trust in God's divine power (Psalm 31:23).

- Seek fellowship with God (Psalm 63:1–8).

- Love God's law (Psalm 119:165).

- Be sensitive to how God feels (Psalm 69:9).

- Love what God loves (Psalm 119:72, 97, 103).

- Love whom God loves (1 John 5:1).

- Hate what God hates (Psalm 97:10).

- Grieve over sin (Matthew 26:75).

- Reject the world (1 John 2:15).

- Long to be with Christ (2 Timothy 4:8).

- Obey God wholeheartedly (John 14:21).

This list barely scratches the surface. The Bible is the source of *everything* Christians need to know to obey God's commands. Once they realize obedience is the only way to demonstrate God's love, they're naturally anxious to understand what God's commands are.

As a new Christian you may already have some sense of the vast wisdom and instruction in God's Word, but feel a little overwhelmed at the sheer magnitude of it. I've been preaching from it for more than forty years, and I'm still overwhelmed. In the next chapter we'll take a look at the Bible and consider, now that we've dedicated our lives to obeying God, how our obedience depends on knowing the Scriptures.

3

FELLOWSHIP OF THE BURNING HEART

According to Luke, on the day of Jesus' resurrection, two men on their way to the village of Emmaus were talking about the astounding events that had just happened. "So it was," he said, "while they conversed and reasoned, that Jesus Himself drew near and went with them. But their eyes were restrained, so that they did not know Him" (Luke 24:15–16). Jesus walked with them without revealing to them who He was, and asked them what they were talking about. They admitted that they were "hoping that it was He [Jesus] who was going to redeem Israel" (verse 21), but that now He was dead, and they thought His plans would go unfulfilled, along with their hopes.

Once they reached the village, the two men invited Jesus to stay with them. As they began to eat, He revealed Himself to them and then vanished from their sight (verses 30–31). The essential point here is the reaction of the men in the next verse: "And they said to one another, 'Did not our heart burn within us while He talked with us on the road, and while He opened the Scriptures to us?'" I like to say they were members of the fellowship of the burning heart. When a true believer hears God's Word, it lights a fire in the heart.

That is certainly the idea behind the Psalms. In many cases the writers' hearts burned for the Word of the Lord. Psalm 1:2 says of a blessed man, "His delight is in the law of the LORD, and in His law he meditates day and night." Psalm 19:10 says God's Word is "more to be desired . . . than gold, yea, than much fine gold; sweeter also than honey and the honeycomb."

There is great joy in understanding God's Word, and even greater joy in obeying it. We've seen that believers have an eagerness to obey God's commands. But to do so, they need to know what those commands are. Everything you need to know to grow in the Christian faith is in the Bible. The Bible is the fountainhead of all spiritual and eternal wisdom and instruction and the source of every good thing.

THE BIBLE IS THE SOURCE OF LIFE

Jesus said, "Man shall not live by bread alone, but by every word that proceeds from the mouth of God" (Matthew 4:4). God's Word provides life and injects it with all that makes you want to live it. Once you begin to direct your life according to the Word of God, life in Christ takes on a full, rich, and exciting meaning.

THE BIBLE IS THE SOURCE OF POWER

As you lift up the Scriptures, you hold in your hand a supernatural resource that has the power to change every area of your life in a way that brings you closer to Christ.

The Power of Conviction. Hebrews 4:12 says, "The word of God is living and powerful, and sharper than any two-edged sword, piercing even to the division of soul and spirit, and of joints and marrow, and is a discerner of the thoughts and intents of the heart." Conviction of sin tells us that something is wrong with our souls the way physical pain tells us something is wrong with our bodies. Nothing pierces to the heart of our sin like God's truth. That's why daily Bible reading and study are so important. When you desire to be all that God wants you to be, you will allow Him to use His Word to penetrate those hidden areas of your life, convict you of your faults, and show you how to repent of them.

The Power of Salvation. In Romans 1:16 Paul tells us, "I am not ashamed of the gospel of Christ, for it is the power of

God to salvation for everyone who believes." The Bible has the power to save us from sin. Therefore it has the power to give us eternal life with God in heaven.

The Power of Transformation. Further on, in chapter 12 of his letter to the church in Rome, Paul says, "I beseech you therefore, brethren, by the mercies of God, that you present your bodies a living sacrifice, holy, acceptable to God, which is your reasonable service. And do not be conformed to this world, but be transformed by the renewing of your mind" (verses 1–2). As you study the Bible and understand its truths, it transforms your thinking. It will begin to wean you off worldly pleasures and cause you to desire godliness. It has the power to separate you from the world's system, pull you away from the love of worldly things, and plant in your heart a love for godly things. Paul called Scripture "the mind of Christ" (1 Corinthians 2:16) because in it is revealed what our Lord thinks. Whoever knows Scripture knows the Lord's thoughts on all that is revealed there.

THE BIBLE IS THE SOURCE OF HAPPINESS

True happiness in life results from the transformation of your thinking processes. Colossians 1:16 says that "all things were created through Him and for Him." That includes you.

Since you were made for God, you won't know true happiness until you know what pleases Him. But you won't know what that is until you know what His manual for living—the Bible—says. As you study His Word and learn to live by His principles, you'll begin to experience great satisfaction and happiness. The prophet Jeremiah realized that when he said, "Your words were found, and I ate them, and Your word was to me the joy and rejoicing of my heart" (Jeremiah 15:16).

When you understand what God wants out of your life and all the promises He has prepared for you, it will bring you joy beyond imagining. Maybe you're having problems in a relationship. Perhaps your home isn't all it ought to be. Maybe you don't have the money to buy something you desperately need. You might be struggling in school or on the job. Even though nothing seems to be working for your good now, I can promise you everything will work out in the end. How can I make a reckless promise like that? Because God's promises in Christ will be fulfilled in you. The Bible says so. And that gives every Christian a reason to rejoice.

THE BIBLE IS THE SOURCE OF MINISTRY

Paul gave Timothy the strategy for reaching others with the truth when he said, "The things that you have heard from me among many witnesses, commit these to faithful men who will be able to teach others also" (2 Timothy 2:2). Just as in a relay race one runner passes the baton to the next, so we pass the baton of God's truth from one to another. Paul committed divine truth to Timothy, and Timothy in turn was to commit that truth to others. Only as you know the Word of God can you pass it on to someone else, who can then do the same thing. In that way the Word spreads throughout the world like ripples across a pond.

THE BIBLE IS THE SOURCE OF TRUTH

We live in the information age. There is nothing you can't find these days on the Internet. Then we have TV, DVD, MP3, and all the rest. Yet what Paul told Timothy two thousand years ago is just as true today: People are "always learning and never able to come to the knowledge of the truth" (2 Timothy 3:7). There's still too much information, and divine wisdom is scarce.

Real truth—God's truth—is life-changing. It changes how you view life, death, time, and eternity. That's because once you are a part of God's family, your perspective on life in this world is based on a heavenly point of view, not an earthly one. Your Bible is the only source of that truth. Jesus prayed to the Father and said, "Your word is truth" (John 17:17). If you want to know about anything—from God to man, from heaven to earth, from past to future, from the intellect to the emotions—it's all in the Bible.

Scripture gives us the answers we can't find on our own. It is divinely revealed truth that fills the vacuum of spiritual ignorance in all of us. Three short verses in Psalm 19:7–9 describe how biblical truth has the authority and sufficiency to answer the important questions of life.

It Is Perfect, Restoring the Soul. Psalm 19:7 says, "The law of the LORD is perfect, converting the soul." *Perfect* comes from a Hebrew word that means "comprehensive" or "complete." That means the Bible contains all the truth necessary to transform and restore the human soul.

The Bible offers hope for all those weighed down by a sense of their own failure. Because it is perfect truth, it can revive man's dead soul and offer new life to those broken by sin and failure. If you are apathetic, Scripture will convict you of sin and show you your real needs. But if you are crushed with emptiness, guilt, and anxiety, God's Word contains truth that can transform your soul with new life in Christ.

It Is Sure and Wise. The psalmist continues, "The testimony of the LORD is sure, making wise the simple" (verse 7). Natural intelligence is at best a leap in the dark. Even the most perceptive philosopher will tell you there is no certainty in human wisdom. At his best, man is totally inadequate in the pursuit of divine truth. God can be known only if He reveals Himself.

I cannot know a person unless that person speaks to me and opens his heart. So with God, He can be known only if He chooses to reveal Himself. And He has. That is what the Bible is—God's self-revelation. God's Word is infallible, totally reliable in every sense. In contrast to human wisdom, which is based on academic pursuit, the Bible can make a simple person wise. All that God wants you to know in life is covered in His Word. It will tell you all you must know to be saved and to grow spiritually, all you need to live and serve God, and even things like how to build lasting friendships, how to develop communication skills, and how to build a solid marriage. All you need is a teachable mind, a receptive spirit, and an obedient heart.

It Is Right, Rejoicing the Heart. In Psalm 19:8 King David wrote, "The statutes of the LORD are right, rejoicing the heart." Everyone wants a happy and contented life. The problem is that we look for joy in all the wrong places. Real happiness cannot be found in pleasure and materialism. People won't find lasting joy in sinful self-gratification and the hedonistic pursuit of money, sex, alcohol, and drugs. Those are all dead ends, as you now know.

God offers real satisfaction only to people who obey His Word. He wants us to be happy. He designed us so that the greatest possible joy comes as a fruit of our obedience to Him.

Best of all, the gladness He gives is not the kind that ends when the party is over. It is a rich, deep joy that operates even in the midst of life's most difficult trials. No matter what pressures you may face in life, He will strengthen and guide you through His Word.

It Is Pure, Enlightening the Eyes. Verse 8 continues, "The commandment of the LORD is pure, enlightening the eyes." Scripture makes sense out of the dark things of life. In a world filled with lying, cheating, murder, war, and tragedy, Scripture helps us understand the depth of man's depravity without God.

What comfort can philosophy offer to someone who loses a child? What can human wisdom say to a person whose spouse has cancer? Only God's Word can speak with authority to the deep needs of life as it enlightens the eyes of those who submit to its truth.

The Bible may not always give easy answers to the hard questions we ask, but the truth it reveals is far superior to the pat answers of human wisdom. Scripture declares the character of God. It shows Him as a loving, caring, all-wise, and omnipotent Sovereign who remains in control no matter how bleak this sin-darkened world may be.

It Is Clean, Enduring Forever. Verse 9 begins, "The fear of the LORD is clean, enduring forever." "The fear of the LORD" is parallel to "the law," "the testimony," "the precepts," and "the commandment" of verses 7–8. It is another of the psalmist's names for Scripture. More than that, "the fear of the LORD" signifies the sum of man's response to God's Word—worship. *Fear* is another word for *worship.*

The Bible, unlike any other book, endures forever. It is relevant in every generation. Though it is an ancient document, it never needs revision. It has been translated into modern languages, but for two millennia it has remained the same in content. Its teachings are never out of date. It speaks to us as pointedly and authoritatively as it ever did to any generation.

Human philosophies come in and out of style, being constantly replaced. Every field of science known to man is in a constant state of flux: changing, growing, discarding one maxim and replacing it with another. But the one thing that never changes is the eternal Word of God.

It Is True and Righteous Altogether. Finally David exclaimed, "The judgments of the LORD are true and righteous altogether" (verse 9). What a bold statement that is! God's Word is true. It's hard today to find anything we can count on for truth. The media, politicians, and even some preachers have a reputation for lacking credibility. In fact, we take it for granted that they regularly distort the truth.

Franz Kafka, the gifted Czech-born writer who lived at the beginning of the twentieth century, used a parable to illustrate the futility of man's search for truth. He described a bombed-out city of rubble where death and ruin were everywhere. People had been crushed under rocks, where they lay dying in agony. In the middle of this total holocaust, one solitary figure sits in a bathroom. Kafka called him the defiant fisherman. He is seated on a toilet seat with a fishing line dangling into a bathtub. There is no water in the tub, and obviously no fish, but the defiant fisherman keeps on fishing anyhow.

That, said Kafka, is what the search for truth is like. It is a worthless, futile pursuit of nonexistent meaning while the whole world is dying all around.

A hopeless picture, yes, and that is what it's like to look for truth apart from the Bible. The natural man cannot find truth in the spiritual realm. He is spiritually dead and unresponsive to God. The only way he can find truth is if the spiritual realm invades the coffin that is his flesh.

That's exactly what the Bible does! It is a supernatural

revelation from God that invades the human heart with the sum of all spiritual truth that we need to know, and it produces righteousness.

THE BIBLE IS THE SOURCE OF GROWTH

Every Christian should want to grow in his relationship to God—to become more Christlike in character. We don't want to be limited in our Christian experience. We want to grow and enjoy the fullness of spiritual life. But that can happen only through daily intake of God's Word. The apostle Peter described the attitude we should have toward our growth through the Bible: "As newborn babes, desire the pure milk of the word, that you may grow thereby" (1 Peter 2:2).

In the Greek, the term translated "long for" refers to an intense, recurring craving, the way babies crave milk. They don't care if it's from a bottle or directly from Mom, what color their room is, or even what time of day it is—they want milk and if they don't get it soon enough, they scream and cry. Believers should have that same kind of single-minded craving for the Word of God.

Peter did not say "read the Bible," or "study" it, or "meditate on it"; he said *desire* it. That's what Paul called "the love of the truth" (2 Thessalonians 2:10). In effect, it produces an attitude in your heart that says, "I want the Word more than I want anything else."

Our desire must be just as strong. Consider the passion for truth outlined in Proverbs:

> My son, if you receive my words, and treasure my commands within you, so that you incline your ear to wisdom, and apply your heart to understanding; yes, if you cry out for discernment, and lift up your voice for understanding, if you seek her as silver, and search for her as for hidden treasures; then you will understand the fear of the LORD, and find the knowledge of God. For the LORD gives wisdom; from His mouth come knowledge and understanding. (2:1–6)

If you seek divine truth as earnestly as some people search after material riches, you will find it, because God has made it available.

Your heavenly Father wants you to grow—by obeying His commands. In the Bible He has given you the resource to know those commands. More than that, His Word is all you need to obey. I pray that your heart will burn for it.

4

THE DAILY BATTLE

*A*ll Christians sin. This may be a shocking admission to people who think being a Christian means being perfect. But if only sinless Christians could go to heaven, heaven would be empty! It's not a reward you can earn; it's a gift of God's grace. Paul made this point in Romans 3:23: "All have sinned and fall short of the glory of God." As Christians, you and I are not exempt from a life in constant conflict with sin, which often leads to disobeying God. No matter how hard we try, we still face a daily battle with sin, and it seems as if sin is always getting the better of us.

TOWARD CHRISTLIKENESS

Scripture recognizes that believers are not perfect. We all fail to achieve God's standard, which is "Be holy, for I am holy" (1 Peter 1:16). Paul saw the sin in his own life, but refused to let it stop him from doing everything he could to overcome it: "Not that I have already attained, or am already perfected; but I press on, that I may lay hold of that for which Christ Jesus has also laid hold of me. Brethren, I do not count myself to have apprehended; but one thing I do, forgetting those things which are behind and reaching forward to those things which are ahead, I press toward the goal for the prize of the upward call of God in Christ Jesus" (Philippians 3:12–14).

In other words, our own imperfection should spur us on toward the goal of complete Christlikeness. Sanctification is the process by which God—working in believers through the Holy Spirit—gradually moves us toward that goal.

It's a gradual transformation. In Romans 12:2, Paul wrote, "Do not be conformed to this world, but be transformed by the renewing of your mind." He also affirmed that sanctification does not end unless "we all come to the unity of the faith and of the knowledge of the Son of God, to a perfect man, to the measure of the stature of the fullness of Christ" (Ephesians 4:13).

The Bible clearly teaches that you can never attain such sinless perfection in this life. Proverbs 20:9 challenges us: "Who can say, 'I have made my heart clean, I am pure from my sin'?" The apostle John affirmed, "If we say that we have no sin, we deceive ourselves, and the truth is not in us" (1 John 1:8). Sanctification is never complete in this lifetime—that will happen only when we are glorified.

The word *sanctify* comes from Hebrew and Greek words that mean "set apart." To be sanctified is to be set apart from sin. At conversion, all believers are released from sin's penalty and set apart unto God. Yet the process of separation from the power of sin in your life has just begun. As you grow in Christ, you become further separated from the influence of sin and more consecrated to God. The sanctification that takes place at conversion initiates a lifelong process of distancing yourself further and further from sin and coming gradually and steadily more into conformity with Christlike righteousness.

The more you become like Christ, the more sensitive you are to the remaining corruptions of the flesh. As you mature in godliness, your sins become both more painful and more obvious. The more you put away sin, the more you will notice sinful tendencies you need to eliminate. That is the paradox of sanctification: the holier you become, the more frustrated you will be by the stubborn remnants of your sin.

More than 150 years ago a dutiful Christian mother explained the idea beautifully to her daughter, who was grieved by her own newly revealed sin. The words are a little old-fashioned, but the message is timeless:

Before His influence was shed into your heart, you could see none of your faults. It was like coming into the parlor some cloudy morning. All the dust and litter of the room would not be visible. But let a bright ray of sunshine gleam in and how you would see every particle of dust! So the Holy Spirit has shined into your heart & you are astonished at what you see there. Do not doubt for a moment His power and His willingness to receive you. He will never leave you or forsake you.

Here on earth, we'll never become sanctified no matter how earnestly we pursue it. But pursue it we will if we are truly born again, for God Himself guarantees our perseverance in righteousness: "May the God of peace Himself sanctify you completely; and may your whole spirit, soul, and body be preserved blameless at the coming of our Lord Jesus Christ" (1 Thessalonians 5:23).

THE DAILY BATTLE WITH SIN

Though he was one of the most spiritual saints who ever lived, and though he was used mightily of God, Paul struggled with personal sin and temptation the same as every other Christian. In Romans 7:14–25 he gives us a vivid description of the battle:

For we know that the law is spiritual, but I am carnal, sold under sin. For what I am doing, I do not understand. For what I will to do, that I do not practice; but what I hate, that I do. If, then, I do what I will not to do, I agree with the law that it is good. But now, it is no longer I who do it, but sin that dwells in me. For I know that in me (that is, in my flesh) nothing good dwells; for to will is present with me, but how to perform what is good I do not find. For the good that I will to do, I do not do; but the evil I will not to do, that I practice. Now if I do what I will not to do, it is no longer I who do it, but sin that dwells in me. I find then a law, that evil is present with me, the one who wills to do good. For I delight in the law of God according to the inward man. But I see another law in my members, warring against the law of my mind, and bringing me into captivity to the law of sin which is in my members. O wretched man that I am! Who will deliver me from this body of death? I thank God—through Jesus Christ our Lord! So then, with the mind I myself serve the law of God, but with the flesh the law of sin.

Paul loved the law of God with his whole heart, yet he found himself wrapped in human flesh and unable to fulfill the righteous law the way his heart wanted to. All true believers should be struggling with the tension Paul described between an ever-increasing hunger for righteousness on the one hand, and a growing sensitivity to sin on the other.

This level of spiritual insight, brokenness, contrition, and humility is the mark of a spiritual and mature believer who has no trust in his own goodness and achievements. It is the lament of a godly Christian who, at the height of spiritual maturity, still finds himself unable to live up to the holy standard. This is the experience of every genuine believer at every stage of spiritual development.

Paul's revealing and heartfelt statement deserves a closer look.

The Flesh Is Frail. Paul said, "I am carnal." A better translation is, "I am of flesh." He was not using *flesh* to refer to his physical body, but to the principle of human frailty, especially our sinful selfishness, which remains with us after salvation until we are ultimately glorified. It is a corruption that permeates and influences every aspect of our being—body, mind, emotions, and will. It is what makes us susceptible to sin even after God makes us partakers of His divine nature (see 2 Peter 1:4). Though sin does not *reign* in us, it nevertheless *remains* in us. "The flesh" is the source and stimulus of our sin.

Unbelievers are said to be "in the flesh" (Romans 8:8–9).

Christians are no longer in the flesh—we are in the Spirit. But we are still "*of* flesh," still fallen humans, and that's the problem: "I know that in me (that is, in my flesh) nothing good dwells . . . So then, with the mind I myself serve the law of God, but with the flesh the law of sin" (Romans 7:18, 25). "Flesh" here refers to our fallenness. It mars all the facets of the total person, including our minds, emotions, and bodies. This residual fallenness—the flesh—is what drags us repeatedly into sin, even though as Christians we hate sin.

Wishing Good Is Easy; Doing Good Is Hard. Every Christian can echo Paul's lament. Yes, God's law is good and we desire to obey it, yet we cannot rid ourselves of sin. We are bound by our own human weakness. Sin is in our very members, and it perpetually frustrates our attempts to obey God perfectly.

Galatians 5:17 says, "The flesh lusts against the Spirit, and the Spirit against the flesh; and these are contrary to one another, so that you do not do the things that you wish." But the previous verse tells us how to win: "Walk in the Spirit, and you shall not fulfill the lust of the flesh" (verse 16). The Holy Spirit gives us the victory.

But that victory seems so slow in coming! Paul wrote, "To will is present with me, but how to perform what is good I do not find. For the good that I will to do, I do not do; but the evil I will not to do, that I practice" (Romans 7:18–19). It's not that Paul was incapable of doing anything right; it's that his *desire* to obey was always greater than his *ability* to obey.

Delight in God's Law. "I find then a law, that evil is present with me, the one who wills to do good. For I delight in the law of God according to the inward man. But I see another law in my members, warring against the law of my mind, and bringing me into captivity to the law of sin which is in my members" (Romans 7:21–23). Paul's inner man, re-created in the likeness of Christ and indwelt by His Spirit, troubled him because he was grieved by the least infraction against God's holy law. He realized how wretchedly short of God's perfect law he lived. Yet in spite of his shortcomings, Paul delighted in God's law. The phrase "in the inner man" could be translated, "from the bottom of my heart." Emanating from the depths of his soul, Paul had a great love for the law of the Lord.

Never Give Up. "O wretched man that I am! Who will deliver me from this body of death? I thank God—through Jesus Christ our Lord! So then, with the mind I myself serve the law of God, but with the flesh the law of sin" (Romans 7:24–25). Christ assures us all of ultimate triumph over the sin in our flesh. Paul said, "We also eagerly wait for the Savior, the Lord Jesus Christ, who will transform our lowly body that it may be conformed to His glorious body" (Philippians 3:20–21). Ours is a triumphant hope!

Yet for now the battle goes on. Full deliverance will come only with glorification. Victory here and now is possible only bit by bit as we kill the deeds of the body through the Holy Spirit: "For if you live according to the flesh you will die; but if by the Spirit you put to death the deeds of the body, you will live" (Romans 8:13).

As one Christian to another, let me warn you that you will be frustrated by your inability to experience the holiness you crave. That is the inevitable experience of every true child of God. In your flesh you will never achieve the level of holiness you want. But press on! Persevere in your faith, and your perseverance will set you apart as a member of the family of God and you will experience what it is to really live in Christ.

CONFESSION OF SIN

Your inability to obey God the way you know you should has an impact on your relationship with Him. Just as a disobedient child disappoints his father, so our sin disappoints our heavenly Father. Yet just as a father welcomes with open arms a child who confesses his disobedience with a repentant spirit, so God restores to us the joy of salvation when we confess our sin to Him (Psalm 51:12).

As part of your new life in Christ, you'll want to maintain that intimate relationship with Him. To do that you need to continually confess your sins to God. As the apostle John explained, "If we confess our sins, He is faithful and just to forgive us our sins and to cleanse us from all unrighteousness" (1 John 1:9). A Christian continually confesses and God continually forgives.

Scripture teaches that redeemed people are to pray regularly for forgiveness. As long as we live in a sinful world and have our own sinful tendencies, there is a sense in which we as Christians, though eternally cleansed, still need daily cleansing from the effects of sin.

You need to forsake your sin regularly, seeking not the pardon of an angry Judge, but the forgiveness of your loving Father—displeased and grieved, yet loving all the same.

True confession of sin is not just admitting you did something wrong, but acknowledging that your sin was against God and in defiance of Him personally. Therefore the primary feature of confession is agreeing with God that you are helplessly guilty. In fact, the Greek word for confession literally means "say the same." To confess your sins is to say the same thing God says about them, acknowledging that God's perspective of your transgressions is correct.

For that reason, true confession also involves repentance—turning away from the evil thought or action. You have not honestly confessed your sins until you have expressed the desire to turn from them. Real confession includes a brokenness that inevitably leads to a change of behavior. In Isaiah 66:2 the Lord says, "On this one will I look: on him who is poor and of a contrite spirit, and who trembles at My word." When you pray, go to God trembling at breaking His Word, longing for victory over your weaknesses and failures.

Confessing your sin, however, does not eliminate God's chastening (disciplining) work in your life. Though you repent, God will often chasten you to correct your behavior in the future. If He chastens you because of sinful behavior, you know you deserve the correction.

When God chastens us as His children, it is for our benefit. Hebrews 12:5–11 says He chastens us as sons so that we might be better sons. Too often believers have the wrong perspective on chastening, wondering why God would allow horrible things to happen to them. Confession allows us to view chastening from God's perspective. Only then can you see how God, through painful results, is shaping you by drawing you away from sin to righteousness.

Yet, our God is a forgiving God. In response and thanks, we confess our sin to Him and turn from it, lest we trample on His grace. If you try to cover your sin, you will not prosper; you will only forfeit your joy and reap divine displeasure.

But when you confess and forsake your sin, there is a guarantee of divine compassion. As wise King Solomon promised in Proverbs 28:13, "He who covers his sins will not prosper, but whoever confesses and forsakes them will have mercy." The God who disciplines sinning saints because of His love for them also delights to shower the brokenhearted and repentant with His mercy.

Sin is a reality of life on earth, but for Christians it is only a temporary, nagging nemesis. A glorious salvation awaits, by the grace of a loving Father who is ready to embrace you forever into His presence, having made you sinless at home in heaven.

5

ANSWERED PRAYER

Praying is like breathing. You don't have to think to breathe, because the atmosphere exerts pressure on your lungs and forces you to do it. When you are adopted into God's family, you enter into a spiritual atmosphere where God's presence and grace exert pressure, or influence, on your life. Prayer is the normal response to that pressure.

We just looked at how a believer who is convicted of his sin will confess his failure to obey God. As a believer, you can't help confessing any more than you can help breathing—the pressure of disappointing God and being separated from intimacy with Him is too great to bear. Most amazing of all, the God of the universe, the Creator, *wants* to answer your prayers.

The apostle John wrote, "Beloved, if our heart does not condemn us, we have confidence toward God. And whatever we ask we receive from Him, because we keep His commandments and do those things that are pleasing in His sight" (1 John 3:21–22). Notice that John said, "If our heart does not condemn us." That refers back to verse 20, which says, "If our heart condemns us, God is greater than our heart, and knows all things." What was John referring to?

God knows the worst that is in us. He sees what's in our hearts, and yet He does not condemn us. That was Paul's point when he said, "There is therefore now no condemnation to those who are in Christ Jesus, who do not walk according to the flesh, but according to the Spirit" (Romans 8:1). Nothing can separate us from the love of God in Christ. In spite of our failure to obey, God knows we long to follow His commands just as He knew of Paul's struggle with sin and his desire to obey.

What we must do to restore the joy of our fellowship with God is confess and repent of our sins. When we have done that, then our hearts, sinful though they are, will not condemn us in His sight. When we are walking in obedience and our consciences are clear because we have confessed our sins, "we have confidence toward God" to rush into His presence. It is then that "whatever we ask we receive from Him, because we keep His commandments and do those things that are pleasing in His sight" (1 John 3:21–22).

The word for "confidence" here means "boldness" or "freedom of speech." John is saying we can go before God with exactly what's on our minds. We have an open relationship with God like a loving child has with his father. We have freedom to ask for whatever is on our hearts and know He will answer us. As Scripture instructs us, "Let us therefore come boldly to the throne of grace, that we may obtain mercy and find grace to help in time of need" (Hebrews 4:16).

QUALIFICATIONS FOR ANSWERED PRAYER

For God to answer prayer, it has to be offered as the Bible instructs. You can't just pray for a new car or a million dollars and expect God to come through like some cosmic Santa Claus. We've already discussed one of the essential qualifications for answered prayer: confession. Psalm 66:18 says, "If I regard iniquity in my heart, the Lord will not hear." If you are harboring unconfessed sin in your life, you need to confess it so you can have that boldness to enter into God's presence. God's Word speaks of other qualifications that are just as important.

Pray According to His Will. John tells us, "This is the confidence that we have in Him, that if we ask anything *according to His will,* He hears us. And if we know that He hears us, whatever we ask, we know that we have the petitions that we have asked of Him" (1 John 5:14–15, emphasis added). Because you have confessed your sin, you can come boldly into

God's presence on any issue as long as it is according to His will.

The word for "hears" means more than just listening to the request; it implies that God is going to give the right answer. You have a blank check, in a sense. But it's a check that can be drawn only on funds deposited in the bank account of God's will. When our desires and requests are aligned with and subjugated to the will of God, we know that He will hear and grant what we seek of Him.

Pray in His Name. Jesus' statement to the disciples on the night He was betrayed carries this incredible promise: "Whatever you ask in My name, that I will do, that the Father may be glorified in the Son. If you ask anything in My name, I will do it" (John 14:13–14). Jesus will do *anything you ask* if you ask according to His will! This was surely a great relief to the disciples, who had left everything and were completely without resources. After Jesus' death they would be alone in a hostile world, yet He assured them they did not need to worry. The gap between Him and them would be closed instantly whenever they prayed. Even though He would be absent, they would have access to all His supplies.

That is not carte blanche for every whim of the flesh. There's a qualifying statement repeated twice for emphasis.

He doesn't say, "I'll give you *absolutely anything* you ask for," but "I'll do what you ask *in My name*." The name of Jesus stands for all that He is. Throughout Scripture, God's names are the same as His attributes. When Isaiah prophesied that Messiah would be called "Wonderful, Counselor, Mighty God, Everlasting Father, Prince of Peace" (9:6), he was not giving Him actual names, but rather an overview of Messiah's character. "I AM WHO I AM," the name revealed to Moses in Exodus 3:14, is as much an affirmation of God's eternal nature as it is a name by which He is to be called.

Therefore, praying in the name of Jesus is more than merely mentioning His name at the end of your prayers. If you truly pray in Jesus' name, you can pray only for that which is consistent with His perfect character, and for that which will bring glory to Him. It implies acknowledgment of all that He has done and a submission to His will.

What praying in Jesus' name really means is that we should pray as if the Lord Himself were doing the asking. We approach the throne of the Father in full identification with the Son, seeking only what He would seek. When we pray with that perspective, we begin to pray for the things that really matter, and we eliminate selfish requests. If we pray that way, He assures us, "I will do it" (John 14:14). That is your guarantee that within His will you will never lack anything.

Pray with a Knowledge of Scripture. Jesus promises, "If you abide in Me, and My words abide in you, you will ask what you desire, and it shall be done for you" (John 15:7). There are two conditions to that promise. First, we must abide. The Greek word for "abide" is in the aorist tense, which indicates something that happened at one point in time and has continuing results. Here "abide" refers to salvation and indicates that the promise is only for real believers.

"My words" does not refer only to the individual words of Christ. The Lord has spoken through the entirety of Scripture; *all* of it is His message to us. Therefore, when He says, "If . . . My words abide in you," He means we must have such high regard for all of Scripture that we let it abide in us, that we hide it in our hearts, and that we commit ourselves to knowing and obeying it. This is the condition for receiving Jesus' promise to give us what we desire. When you are controlled by His Word, you are not going to ask anything against God's will. Because you want what God wants, you are guaranteed answers to your prayers.

THE DESIRES OF YOUR HEART

As Paul expressed in 2 Corinthians 10, "[We are] casting down arguments and every high thing that exalts itself against the knowledge of God, bringing every thought into captivity to the obedience of Christ" (verse 5). You must rid your mind of everything that violates God's truth and will. By cultivating an intimate love relationship with Christ, you will desire what He desires; then whatever you ask, you will receive. The psalmist said, "Delight yourself also in the LORD, and He shall give you the desires of your heart" (Psalm 37:4). When you delight completely in the Lord, His desires become your own. And they will never go unfulfilled.

6

THE SUPREME TEST

So far, we've spent our time considering how your life as a Christian is transformed by your relationship with God, His Son, and His Spirit. Now let's look at ways you can expect your life to be different in relation to the people around you, believers and unbelievers alike.

In chapter 1 we focused on what Jesus identified as God's greatest commandment: "You shall love the LORD your God with all your heart, with all your soul, with all your strength, and with all your mind" (Luke 10:27). In the same verse He also said to love "your neighbor as yourself." What is your Christian responsibility to love your neighbor in general, and fellow Christians in particular?

Loving your neighbor as yourself involves the same virtue as loving the Lord with all your being; there's no difference in sincerity, commitment, or dedication. It is by choice—intentional and active—not merely sentimental and emotional. And it is measured, Jesus said, by love for "yourself." If you're hungry, you feed yourself; when you're thirsty, you get a drink; and when you're sick, you take medicine or see a doctor—all because you are consumed with caring for *yourself.* You don't just think or talk about what you need; if you have the power to meet your needs you meet them. A Christian looks out for others with the same level of attention and effort.

This dual command sums up the basic requirement of Judaism as well as Christianity: to love God and to love your fellow man. Jesus said, "On these two commandments hang all the Law and the Prophets" (Matthew 22:40). Everything God required of believers in both the Old and New Testaments is based on them.

The apostle John talked about love for one another throughout his first epistle:

> Brethren, I write no new commandment to you, but an old commandment which you have had from the beginning. The old commandment is the word which you heard from the beginning. Again, a new commandment I write to you, which thing is true in Him and in you, because the darkness is passing away, and the true light is already shining. He who says he is in the light, and hates his brother, is in darkness until now. He who loves his brother abides in the light, and there

is no cause for stumbling in him. But he who hates his brother is in darkness and walks in darkness, and does not know where he is going, because the darkness has blinded his eyes. (1 John 2:7–11)

John was saying that love is an essential test of our salvation. Light and darkness represent eternal life and eternal death. The guarantee is that "he who loves his brother abides in the light."

AN OLD COMMANDMENT

John's characterization of an "old commandment" tells us this teaching is not some new truth his audience had never heard before. Since the majority of the first converts to Christianity were Jews, they knew that in the Old Testament God established the law of love in unmistakable terms. We noted in the first chapter their familiarity with the Shema. Just as important to them was Leviticus 19:18, which says, "You shall love your neighbor as yourself: I am the LORD." So news of their responsibility to love their neighbors was no surprise.

The apostle Paul built on that truth:

Owe no one anything except to love one another, for he who loves another has fulfilled the law. For the commandments, "You shall not commit adultery," "You shall not murder," "You shall not steal," "You shall not bear false witness," "You shall not covet," and if there is any other commandment, are all summed up in this saying, namely, "You shall love your neighbor as yourself." Love does no harm to a neighbor; therefore love is the fulfillment of the law. (Romans 13:8–10)

Paul quoted Leviticus 19:18 to show that loving your neighbor isn't just a part of the Law; it fulfills the Law. It encompasses all of God's laws concerning human relationships. If you truly love your neighbor, you'll do for him only what is in his best interests.

The prohibition against adultery in Scripture is clear, but if you love your wife, you won't be tempted to be adulterous in the first place. And you won't violate your neighbor's trust if you love him. The same is true with all of the commands Paul mentions. You're not going to steal from someone you love, lie to someone you love, or covet something that belongs to someone you love. The link between loving your neighbor and obeying God is inseparable.

When a person comes to Christ, he must count the cost of becoming a Christian. He needs to know there is a commitment to obedience, to the law of God, and to love for God and His people. So the command to love ought to be clear from the beginning because it is part of the covenant of obedience you take when you become a Christian: you will obey the lordship of Jesus Christ, and that means you will love the brethren. God will work in you so your obedience is not burdensome and your love won't be forced or superficial.

A NEW COMMANDMENT

What John said in 1 John 2:8 appears to contradict the "old commandment" mentioned in verse 7: "Again, a new commandment I write to you, which thing is true in Him and in you, because the darkness is passing away, and the true light is already shining." Actually, this new commandment is the same as the old one—John is just giving it a new spin. It's not new in time, but in quality and character.

Manifest in Christ. The newness of the command that "is true in Him" is truly manifest (meaning clearly shown or readily apparent) in Jesus Christ. Never before, in spite of all the clear teaching throughout the Old Testament, has there been an embodiment of that love as clearly manifest in all its perfection as in Jesus Christ. Only our Lord could show the world what perfect love is. All others fall miserably short of the standard. So the newness isn't in the command; it's in Christ.

Luke's account of an event the night before our Lord's

crucifixion is an ideal example of how Jesus manifested His love. As He and His twelve disciples prepared to eat the Passover meal, "there was also a dispute among them, as to which of them should be considered the greatest" (22:24).

If any one of the dozen men bickering there in the Upper Room should have been thinking about the glory that was rightfully his, it was Jesus. Yet, John said, "Now before the Feast of the Passover, when Jesus knew that His hour had come that He should depart from this world to the Father, having loved His own who were in the world, He loved them to the end" (John 13:1). "To the end" means He loved them "to perfection." He loved them to the uttermost. He loved them with total fullness of love. That is the nature of Christ's love. At the moment when anyone else would have been totally concerned with self, Jesus, who of all those present had the most right to claim superiority, selflessly humbled Himself to meet the needs of others. Genuine love is like that.

Jesus waited until everyone was seated and supper was served. In a time when roads were dusty and people typically wore sandals, hosts were traditionally responsible for washing their guests' feet. This unpleasant task was usually performed by the lowliest slave in the household. Etiquette dictated that it be done before the meal, but for some reason no servant was available that day. Yet how could disciples destined for greatness perform such a menial and humble duty?

In an unforgettable act of humility that must have stunned the disciples, "Jesus, knowing that the Father had given all things into His hands, and that He had come from God and was going to God, rose from supper and laid aside His garments, took a towel and girded Himself. After that, He poured water into a basin and began to wash the disciples' feet, and to wipe them with the towel with which He was girded" (John 13:3–5).

With calmness and majesty, perhaps saying nothing, Jesus stood up, took a pitcher of water, and poured the water into a basin. He then removed His outer robe, His belt, and very likely His inner tunic—leaving Him clothed like a slave—put a towel around His waist, and knelt to wash the feet of His disciples, one by one.

To go from being God in glory (verse 3) to washing the feet of sinful disciples (verses 4–5) is a long step—yet a step bathed in humility and brimming with the manifestation of perfect love. John wrote, "Let us not love in word or in tongue, but in deed and in truth" (1 John 3:18). Love that is real is love expressed in action, not just words.

Manifest in Believers. Not only is this new commandment "true in Him," but also "in you" (1 John 2:8). For the first time perfect love is manifest in Christ, and now it has been manifest in us in dimensions no one has ever seen before.

That's the glorious realization of what it means to be a new creation in Christ.

On the same night Jesus provided such a wonderful example of love, He told the disciples: "I will pray the Father, and He will give you another Helper, that He may abide with you forever—the Spirit of truth, whom the world cannot receive, because it neither sees Him nor knows Him; but you know Him, for He dwells with you and will be in you" (John 14:16–17). While clearly the Holy Spirit has been with all who ever believed throughout redemptive history as the source of truth, faith, and life, Jesus indicates that something new is coming in His ministry. When the Holy Spirit comes "in you," you will have the capacity to love God, Christ, and all others.

When you became a Christian—a member of God's family—the Holy Spirit took up residence in your life. Romans 5:5 says, "The love of God has been poured out in our hearts by the Holy Spirit who was given to us." God deposits His incredible love within us, giving us the capacity to love others. Paul wrote, "But concerning brotherly love you have no need that I should write to you, for you yourselves are taught by God to love one another" (1 Thessalonians 4:9). As new creations in Christ, as children of God, Christians love each other.

If God lives in you, if you share His life, you will also love, because "God is love" (1 John 4:8). This is not just a responsibility; it is evidence of God's presence and your changed life. It is impossible for a true believer not to love other believers.

The apostle Peter added, "Since you have purified your souls in obeying the truth through the Spirit in sincere love of the brethren, love one another fervently with a pure heart" (1 Peter 1:22). That is characteristic of a true believer—it is who you are: you obeyed the truth, your soul was cleansed, and that produced a genuine love for the brethren. The command to love one another is based on your new capacity to love, and you are to do so fervently. The Greek word for "fervently" was used to refer to a muscle stretched to its limit. The idea is, you ought to love one another to the max.

If you don't have a love for God's people, for the members of your new family in Christ, that's clear evidence you're still a product of your sinful self, separated from the life and love of God. If you are a true Christian, the proof will be in your love. Though it will be an imperfect effort, you'll do everything in your power to exhibit a heart of love, not of hatred. Your desire will be to serve others, not make demands on them; to help others, not harm them; to encourage others, not tear them down; to love others as you love yourself and as God your Creator loves you—a love so total and complete that He sacrificed His only Son that you might live and love forever.

7

OLD FRIENDS,
NEW FRIENDS

*L*oving other Christians is proof of the change God has wrought in your heart. But there's also another proof, perhaps the severest trial you will face as a new believer: people who were once your friends, maybe even members of your earthly family, may now hate you the way the world hated Christ.

On the night before the Crucifixion, Jesus warned His closest friends, His disciples, about what they could expect from the world of men. In spite of the wonderful, divine promises that would be fulfilled in their lives, life would be far from blissful. Ministry would not be easy in a rebellious, Christ-hating world. The world was going to treat them the same way it treated Him, and they were going to be despised and persecuted—some of them even brutally killed.

These things I command you, that you love one another. If the world hates you, you know that it hated Me before it hated you. If you were of the world, the world would love its own. Yet because you are not of the world, but I chose you out of the world, therefore the world hates you. Remember the word that I said to you, "A servant is not greater than his master." If they persecuted Me, they will also persecute you. If they kept My word, they will keep yours also. But all these things they will do to you for My name's sake, because they do not know Him who sent Me. If I had not come and spoken to them, they would have no sin, but now they have no excuse for their sin. He who hates Me hates My Father also. If I had not done among them the works which no one else did, they would have no sin; but now they have seen and also hated both Me and My Father. But this happened that the word might be fulfilled which is written in their law, "They hated Me without a cause." (John 15:17–25)

One reason their love for one another was so important was that they would know hatred from the world. Love among Christians was the only genuine love they would know.

History shows that Jesus was right; the apostles were hated. James was martyred. The Roman emperor Nero beheaded Paul. Andrew persisted in preaching and was tied to a cross and crucified. Peter, too, was crucified; tradition holds that he was crucified upside down because he considered himself unworthy of the same death as his Savior. All of them were martyred except perhaps Matthew and John, the latter being exiled to the Isle of Patmos. The rest of Christ's followers suffered persecution from the Roman government, which regarded them as disloyal citizens and a threat to the unity of the empire.

Following Christ isn't likely to lead you to martyrdom or exile, but the same hostility toward believers is true in today's world. The culture does not accept Christians because it rejects the gospel of our Lord. And you can't evade that hostility without compromising your Christianity. That means to continue following Christ, you have to accept the fact that others will resent you, including some who have loved you in the past.

Jesus gives three reasons why persecution is unavoidable for you as a Christian:

YOU ARE NOT OF THE WORLD

The world rejects Jesus' disciples because they are no longer a part of its system. Jesus told the apostles, "If you were of the world, the world would love its own. Yet because you are not of the world, but I chose you out of the world, therefore the world hates you" (John 15:19). "World" is the English translation of *kosmos*, a common word in Greek. It appears often in John's writings and changes its meaning with the context. Here it means the evil, sinful system begun by Satan and acted out by men. The *kosmos* is the result and expression of human depravity. It is set against Christ, His people, and His kingdom, and Satan and his evil minions control it.

This evil world system is incapable of genuine love. When Jesus said the world loves its own, He was saying that a worldly individual loves himself and his own things. He loves others only if it is to his advantage. The world's love is always selfish and superficial.

The world sets itself against those who love and follow Jesus, those who declare their faith in Him and show it by their words and deeds. It does not generally persecute those who are part of its system. Jesus said to His earthly brothers who did not follow Him during His ministry, "The world cannot hate you, but it hates Me because I testify of it that its works are evil" (John 7:7).

The unavoidable fact is that people who don't know Jesus Christ are part of a system that is anti-God, anti-Christ, and satanic. That system fights against God and His principles and is opposed to all that is good, godly, and Christlike. Part of that system is false religion. While the majority of people appear religious, their religion is not the same as righteousness. False religions and their followers have a superficial tolerance of the things of God. Still, they are tools of Satan in his war against the truth. They disguise themselves with godliness, but they reveal their true nature by suppressing the truth. Throughout history, false religion has been the most aggressive opponent of the true church.

Persecution is inevitable for the righteous. Paul warned Timothy, "Yes, and all who desire to live godly in Christ Jesus will suffer persecution" (2 Timothy 3:12). The true believer stands apart from the world because he has been made holy through identification with Jesus Christ. He lives righteously and does not belong to the system. Because a genuine Christian represents God and Christ, Satan uses the world's system to attack him. That is why Jesus prayed for the Father's protection of His followers: "I do not pray that You should take them out of the world, but that You should keep them from the evil one" (John 17:15).

Our lives are to be a rebuke to the sinful world. Ephesians 5:11 says, "And have no fellowship with the unfruitful works of darkness, but rather expose them." If you are not experiencing much rejection from the world, your life may not be a rebuke to the world. To have an impact for Christ on this hostile and perverted world, you must avoid sin and "become blameless and harmless, children of God without fault in the midst of a crooked and perverse generation, among whom you shine as lights in the world" (Philippians 2:15).

That was Jesus' point in Matthew 5:14–16, "You are the light of the world. A city that is set on a hill cannot be hidden. Nor do they light a lamp and put it under a basket, but on a lampstand, and it gives light to all who are in the house. Let your light so shine before men, that they may see your good works and glorify your Father in heaven." Make sure your righteousness is visible to the world; don't hide it through compromise or a tolerance of sin.

You stand out from the world because Jesus has chosen you for that. In John 15:19 He says, "I chose you out of the world." Jesus is literally saying, "I chose you for Myself." He has chosen you to be different. So be the living rebuke to the rest of the world that Christ called you to be.

THE WORLD HATES CHRIST

A second reason persecution is inevitable for Christians is that the world hates the Lord Jesus. Jesus told the Eleven, "Remember the word that I said to you, 'A servant is not greater than his master.' If they persecuted Me, they will also persecute you. If they kept My word, they will keep yours also" (John 15:20). Because the world hates Him, it hates those of us who name Him as Lord.

Not everyone rejects Christ, and not everyone will reject us. A few will listen and believe. Yet much of the world's apparent acceptance of Jesus is nothing more than a facade. Most of the movies, songs, and books about Jesus written from a secular viewpoint only confuse and deceive people into thinking they understand the truth about Him. But no one can really know Him without knowing about sin, repentance, judgment, and salvation.

There was a time in Western history when Christianity became the only acceptable religion. After two centuries of intense persecution, the Roman government suddenly adopted it. Christianity became the official religion of the Roman Empire, and everyone had to be a "Christian." True Christianity was endangered more by shallow popularity than it had been by persecution. Infant baptism was adopted as the means to "Christianize" everyone. Christianity had become a monstrosity, an institutionalized blasphemy, and it became unclear just what constituted genuine saving faith. Satan welcomes that kind of confusion as much as he relishes persecuting the church.

There is a unique joy in being so fully identified with Jesus Christ that you suffer the rebuke, ridicule, and hatred directed at Him. Most Christians never know that joy. In Philippians 3:10, Paul called it "the fellowship of His sufferings." First Peter 2:21 says, "For to this you were called, because Christ also suffered for us, leaving us an example, that you should follow His steps." But when we share His sufferings, we also share His joy over those who come to saving faith. And that makes all the sacrifices worthwhile.

THE WORLD DOES NOT KNOW GOD

Jesus gave the disciples another reason for persecution: "But all these things they will do to you for My name's sake, because they do not know Him who sent Me" (John 15:21). The Jews of Jesus' day prided themselves on what they thought was an in-depth knowledge of God. When Jesus said that they did not know God at all, the religious leaders were infuriated. But in rejecting Christ they themselves proved He was right. They claimed to know God, yet they hated Christ, who was God in human flesh. Their love for God was a pretense.

What many people fail to realize is that religion itself is perhaps the greatest hindrance to the knowledge of the true God. The world's approach to religion is to postulate a god and worship it, even though that god does not exist outside man's imagination. Jesus exposed the false religion propounded by the Jewish leaders when He said, "You are of your father the devil, and the desires of your father you want to do" (John 8:44).

The problem is not that men have no access to the truth about God. Romans 1:19 says, "Because what may be known of God is manifest in them, for God has shown it to them."

Through both innate knowledge and nature, God gives everyone basic knowledge that He exists. People willfully reject the truth, not because of ignorance but because they love the darkness rather than the light. Exposing men to the truth is like shining a light on the bug that just wants to crawl back into the darkness.

People in Jesus' time knew what the Old Testament taught about the Messiah. They also heard what Christ said and saw what He did. But the Jewish leaders in the Sanhedrin, along with the people of Israel, and the Romans, killed Him anyway. Jesus quoted Psalm 69:4 in John 15:25: "They hated Me without a cause." The people's rejection of Him was a fulfillment of David's words. Jesus had healed all manner of diseases; He had fed multitudes; He had been completely sinless. How could anyone hate Him?

The world hated Jesus because He exposed its sin. When His divine holiness cast its righteous light on those of the world, it exposed their love of darkness. Instead of turning to Him in faith and love, they turned against Him in unbelief and hatred.

The evil system of the world is no different today—it still hates Jesus. And it still hates those who truly serve Him. As a follower of Christ, you will have to suffer the hatred of the world. Paul warns us that suffering persecution is the lot of "all who desire to live godly in Christ Jesus" (2 Timothy 3:12).

And yet, to be persecuted for Him is a unique privilege (see Acts 5:41; Philippians 3:10). And when you truly suffer for righteousness' sake—family and friends turn against you, and you are hated without cause—you will then begin to understand persecution, not as a trial to be resisted or avoided, but as a wonderful privilege to be welcomed and embraced and shared with all who are your family in Christ.

8

A SPIRITUAL HARVEST

The Bible often refers to God as our heavenly Father and Christians as a family. Another frequent biblical image is of Jesus as a vine and Christians as branches: we grow through the nurturing of Christ and bear spiritual fruit as the result of His Spirit's infusing us. This vine-and-branches concept is an ideal metaphor for the Christian life. As a branch is nothing apart from the vine, so we can do nothing apart from Christ. A branch draws all of its strength from the vine, and we become strong by drawing from His strength.

In John 15, Christ is the Vine and the Father is the Vinedresser. The Father prunes the fruit-bearing branches to make them bear more fruit, removing and burning fruitless branches so that the fruitfulness of the vine is increased. The branches that abide in the Vine—those who are truly in Christ—are blessed; they grow and bear fruit, and the Father lovingly tends them.

Jesus told the disciples, "Abide in Me, and I in you. As

the branch cannot bear fruit of itself, unless it abides in the vine, neither can you, unless you abide in Me" (verse 4). Whoever abides discovers that his soul is nourished with the truths of God as he stays in a close, living, energized relationship with Jesus Christ. The natural result is spiritual fruit.

Don't ever think you can bear spiritual fruit alone. In nature, a branch can bear no fruit apart from its vine. Even the strongest branches, cut off from the vine, become more helpless than the weakest. Similarly, spiritual fruit bearing is not a matter of being strong or weak, good or bad, brave or cowardly, clever or foolish, experienced or inexperienced. Whatever your gifts, accomplishments, or virtues, they cannot produce fruit if you are detached from Jesus Christ.

To bear genuine fruit, you must get as close to the true Vine, our Lord Jesus Christ, as you can. Strip away all the things of the world. Put aside the sins that distract you and sap your energy, and everything that robs you of a deep, personal, loving relationship with Jesus. Stay in God's Word. Having done all that, don't worry about bearing fruit. It is not your concern. Get close to Jesus Christ, and His energy in you will produce fruit.

Fruit is a frequent metaphor in Scripture. The main word for it is used approximately a hundred times in the Old Testament and seventy times in the New Testament. It is mentioned often, yet also often misunderstood. Fruit is not outward success. It's a common misconception to think that if a ministry is big, it is fruitful. But a church or Bible study group isn't successful just because it attracts a crowd. The whole church could be spiritually dead, while missionaries preaching to a handful of spiritually hungry listeners bear much fruit. Infectious enthusiasm or a winsome personality might produce a rollicking celebration full of happy people, but they have nothing to do with spiritual fruit. God produces real fruit in our lives when we abide in Him.

What kind of fruit brings glory to God? Philippians 1:11 says, "Being filled with the fruits of righteousness which are by Jesus Christ, to the glory and praise of God." Righteousness is the fruit God desires in our lives. Yet it is God who produces the fruit of righteousness within us so that He may be glorified.

There are two basic kinds of fruit—two ways in which your life can make an impact on others.

ATTITUDE FRUIT

The apostle Paul wrote in Galatians 5:22–23, "But the fruit of the Spirit is love, joy, peace, longsuffering, kindness, goodness, faithfulness, gentleness, self-control. Against such there is no law." Those were all traits of our Lord. And if those attitudes are characteristic of your life, the fruit of active good works will follow.

Love. The first character of spiritual fruit is love, which we looked at in detail in chapter 6. We are to love God with all our hearts, souls, minds, and strength, and love our neighbors as ourselves (see Luke 10:25–28). Loving God is the greatest commandment.

Joy. This is the deep-down sense of well-being that comes from knowing all is well between you and God. It is not a result of favorable circumstances, but is God's gift to believers. Joy is a part of God's own nature and Spirit that He manifests in His children. While it is a gift to us, we're also commanded to "rejoice in the Lord always" (Philippians 4:4), gratefully accepting and reveling in this supreme blessing we already possess.

Peace. If joy is exhilaration from being right with God, then peace is the tranquillity of mind that results from the saving relationship. Like joy, peace is not based on circumstances. Christians "know that all things work together for good to those who love God, to those who are the called according to His purpose" (Romans 8:28). God is in control of your life, no matter what your circumstances may be from a human perspective. That is why Jesus could say without qualification to those who trusted in Him, "Let not your heart be troubled" (John 14:1). There is no reason for you to be afraid.

Longsuffering (or Patience). If you have patience, you are able to endure with tolerance and longsuffering the injuries inflicted by others, and you can accept irritating or painful situations with a calm willingness. God Himself is slow to anger (Psalm 86:15 NASB) and expects His children to be the same. It's important that you emulate the Lord's patience: "as the elect of God, holy and beloved, put on . . . longsuffering" (Colossians 3:12), especially with believers, "bearing with one another in love" (Ephesians 4:2).

Kindness. This is tender concern for others. It has nothing to do with weakness or lack of conviction but is the genuine desire to treat others gently, just as the Lord treats you. Paul reminded the Thessalonians that even though he was an apostle, he was "gentle among [them], just as a nursing mother cherishes her own children" (1 Thessalonians 2:7). He admonished Timothy not to "quarrel," but to "be gentle to all" (2 Timothy 2:24).

Goodness. This refers to moral and spiritual excellence characterized by sweetness and active kindness. Paul said, "As we have opportunity, let us do good to all, especially to those who are of the household of faith" (Galatians 6:10). To the Thessalonians he wrote, "We also pray always for you that our God would count you worthy of this calling, and fulfill all the good pleasure of His goodness and the work of faith with power" (2 Thessalonians 1:11).

Faithfulness. This pertains to loyalty and trustworthiness. Jeremiah declared that the Lord's "compassions fail not. They are new every morning; great is Your faithfulness" (Lamentations 3:22–23). We, too, ought to "be found faithful" (1 Corinthians 4:2).

Gentleness. This is better translated *meekness.* The New Testament term for *meekness* is used to describe three attitudes: submissiveness to the will of God (Colossians 3:12), teachableness (James 1:21), and consideration of others (Ephesians 4:2). Although He was God, Jesus was "gentle and lowly in heart" on earth (Matthew 11:29). Like our Lord, we are to actively pursue meekness and gentleness (1 Timothy 6:11) and to wear them like a garment (Colossians 3:12).

Self-Control. A believer who exercises self-control restrains his passions and appetites. In His incarnation Christ was the epitome of self-control. He was never tempted or tricked into doing or saying anything that was not consistent with His Father's will and His own divine nature. Like Jesus, we should "add to [our] faith . . . self-control" (2 Peter 1:5–6).

These Christlike characteristics come only from the Holy Spirit. He establishes and ripens them in us, not sequentially—first loving, then once we have become loving, joyful, and so on—but together as part of our lives as we abide in Christ.

ACTION FRUIT

The fruit of godly attitudes leads to the fruit of godly actions and offerings to God.

Thankful Praise. Hebrews 13:15 says, "Therefore by Him let us continually offer the sacrifice of praise to God, that is, the fruit of our lips, giving thanks to His name." When you praise God and thank Him for who He is and what He has done, you offer Him fruit.

Help to Those in Need. Members of the Philippian church gave Paul a gift, and he told them he was glad for their sakes that they had: "Not that I seek the gift, but I seek the fruit that abounds to your account" (Philippians 4:17). He appreciated it not for the sake of the gift, but for the fruit of lovingkindness in their lives that it represented. In Romans 15:28, Paul wrote "Therefore, when I have performed this and have sealed to them this fruit, I shall go by way of you to Spain." Again he referred to a gift as "fruit." A gift to someone in need is fruit if it is offered from a loving heart, in the divine energy of the indwelling Christ.

Purity in Conduct. Paul wanted Christians to be holy in their behavior. He encouraged the Colossians to "walk worthy of the Lord, fully pleasing Him, being fruitful in every good work and increasing in the knowledge of God" (Colossians 1:10).

Converts. New believers in Christ are the fruits of prayer, witnessing, and living a godly example. Paul called the first converts in Achaia the "the firstfruits of Achaia" in 1 Corinthians 16:15. (See also Daniel 12:3; John 4:36; Romans 6:22; 1 Corinthians 3:5–9.) Like other spiritual fruit, the key to a successful harvest here is how faithfully you abide in Christ yourself. You'll never win converts by anxiously keeping up a flurry of "evangelistic activities." Concentrate on your relationship with Jesus Christ and He will give you opportunities to share your faith. There is no need to become anxious because you haven't won a certain number of people to Christ. As you become closer to Him and more like Him, you will discover that telling others the gospel is an outgrowth of abiding. You may not always see fruit immediately, but you will bear it nevertheless.

When Jesus was traveling to Samaria, He met a woman at a well. She told the people in her town about Jesus. As the people from the town came out to meet Him, He said to the disciples:

> Do you not say, "There are still four months and then comes the harvest"? Behold, I say to you, lift up your eyes and look at the fields, for they are already white for harvest! And he who reaps receives wages, and gathers fruit for eternal life, that both he who sows and he who reaps may rejoice together, For in this the saying is true: "One sows and another reaps." I sent you to reap that for which you have not labored; others have labored, and you have entered into their labors. (John 4:35–38)

The disciples were reaping the results of the labor of other workers. Those people did not see all the results of their labor, but their efforts still bore fruit.

Modern missions pioneer William Carey spent thirty-five years in India before he saw one convert. Some people think he had a fruitless ministry. But almost every convert in India to this day is fruit on his branch, because he translated the New Testament into many different Indian dialects. Carey was not the one to directly reap what he had sown, but his life bore much fruit.

You often can't gauge the impact your life has on others. But you can be sure that as you develop godly attitudes, godly actions will result, and that God's kingdom will continue to be enriched by your spiritual fruit according to His perfect will.

9

DON'T JUST SIT THERE

When you learn some especially exciting news, don't you want to jump right up and tell everyone you know? I know I do. It's only human nature. Well, as a Christian, you now know the greatest, most incredible news in history: God sent His perfect Son to die for the sins of the world, and all who believe in Him will live forever in heaven.

So don't just sit there; tell others!

Tell them by the way you graciously accept criticism or disappointment. Tell them by the way you humbly acknowledge success. Tell them by the way you answer a question about your faith. Tell them by remaining true to the commands of Christ, loving your enemies, or bearing the unmistakable fruit of the Spirit. But tell them! And then be ready to speak to them the truth of Christ.

In the same way that we are God's spiritual children—branches of His one true Vine—we represent the body of Christ, and He is our Head. When Christ walked the earth,

He manifested love, holiness, wisdom, power, and all the authority of God. Christians, as members of the body of Christ, are to reflect those attributes to the world.

We read that God has predestined believers to be conformed to the image of His Son (Romans 8:28–29). Think about the miraculous nature of that statement. Christ takes our human bodies, which are physically frail and subject to sin and death, and makes them into His temple—literally dwelling in them, planting in them His glory, that they might manifest Him to the world.

Therefore, every member of the Body can and should be a witness. "You shall receive power," said Jesus, "when the Holy Spirit has come upon you; and you shall be witnesses" (Acts 1:8). Jesus also said, "Go therefore and make disciples of all the nations, baptizing them in the name of the Father and of the Son and of the Holy Spirit, teaching them to observe all things that I have commanded you; and lo, I am with you always, even to the end of the age" (Matthew 28:19–20). There is no waiver given, no excuse accepted. "Therefore, if anyone is in Christ, he is a new creation; old things have passed away; behold, all things have become new. Now all things are of God, who has reconciled us to Himself through Jesus Christ, and has given us the ministry of reconciliation" (2 Corinthians 5:17–18). Anyone reconciled to Christ has the ministry of telling others about Him.

We are not citizens of this earth, because "our citizenship is in heaven" (Philippians 3:20). We belong to a different realm, yet we live in the world and are called to be ambassadors, telling the people of this perishing world that they, too, can be reconciled to the King of kings, and that He desires to make them subjects of His eternal kingdom.

This doesn't mean you have to witness by preaching on street corners—though I can tell you from firsthand experience that it's an unforgettable adventure. Your witness may be by example, or something you write one day, or take any number of other forms. But however it happens, don't worry about whether or not you'll do a good job. Just remember that the Holy Spirit empowers us—individually and as a body—to witness: "When the Helper comes, whom I shall send to you from the Father, the Spirit of truth who proceeds from the Father, He will testify of Me. And you also will bear witness, because you have been with Me from the beginning" (John 15:26–27).

ON TRIAL

In those two verses we discover the basic concept of our *witness*. The very word takes us into a law court. We see a judge on the bench and a prisoner on trial. We hear the case argued by the prosecution, then by the defense. Both call witnesses to substantiate their arguments. The setting implies that Christians are witnesses in a trial, so to speak. Jesus Christ is on trial. The judge is the world. The defense attorney is the Holy Spirit. The prosecutor is Satan.

The world judges Christ based on witnesses. Some people judge Him to be a fake; some, a good man; others, a moral teacher; still others, a liar; and so on. If a witness tears down the claims of Jesus Christ by the kind of life he lives, it would be better if he were out of the courtroom altogether. He only confuses the issue. The Holy Spirit defends Christ through the members of the Body who witness and confirm by their lives the testimony of Christ (John 15:27). Thus all Christians are witnesses, either helping or hindering the cause of Christ.

God's Word sets forth five positive aspects of our witness: it is to the world, of the Son, by the Father, through the Holy Spirit, and in the Body.

Witness Is to the World. As we discovered in chapter 7, the world hates Christians. It ostracizes them and even kills them. The world is also antagonistic to the gospel. But Jesus said believers must witness to such hostility: "When the Helper comes," you will confront the world and witness to it.

How should you react when you are faced with the opposition of the world? Should you retaliate in anger or withdraw in self-pity? No! You are to bear witness before the world whatever the cost—and count it all joy to suffer in Christ's place (James 1:2).

Witness Is of the Son. John 15:27 declares, "You also will bear witness, because you have been with Me." Christ is on trial, and a Christian's testimony must be of Him.

Preaching centers on Jesus Christ throughout the New Testament. The apostle John describes himself as one "who bore witness to the word of God, and to the testimony of Jesus Christ" (Revelation 1:2). Testimony is always directly associated with Jesus Christ. In fact, we even read that the Old Testament witnessed of Him: "For the testimony of Jesus is the spirit of prophecy" (Revelation19:10).

The apostles had no doubts that they were to witness of the Son. Jesus told them, "You shall be witnesses to Me" (Acts 1:8). Their sermons in the early church were always about Him, as when Peter preached to Cornelius and said:

The word which God sent to the children of Israel, preaching peace through Jesus Christ—He is Lord of all—that word you know, which was proclaimed throughout all Judea, and began from Galilee after the baptism which John preached: how God anointed Jesus of Nazareth with the Holy Spirit and with power, who went about doing good and healing all who were oppressed by the devil, for God was with Him. And we are witnesses of all the things which He did both in the land of the Jews and in Jerusalem, whom they killed by hanging on a tree. Him God raised up on the third day, and showed Him openly. (Acts 10:36–40)

Biblical witnessing is a testimony to Jesus Christ. It is proclaiming the great truths of His virgin birth, sinless life, atoning death, physical resurrection, bodily ascension, and coming again.

Witness Is by the Father. When Jesus Christ sent the Holy Spirit, He sent God's witness to this world: "When the Helper comes, whom I shall send to you from the Father, the Spirit of truth who proceeds from the Father, He will testify of Me" (John 15:26). It was the Father's supreme concern to bring honor and glory to the Son, and the Spirit helped Him. Jesus answered the Jews' question about His identity by saying, "If I honor Myself, My honor is nothing. It is My Father who honors Me" (John 8:54).

The Father bore witness to the Son first through the Old Testament. "You search the Scriptures," Jesus said to the Jews, "for in them you think you have eternal life; and these are they which testify of Me" (John 5:39). Jesus revealed additional things about the Old Testament witness to Himself as He spoke to two of His disciples on the road to Emmaus: "And beginning at Moses and all the Prophets, He expounded to them in all the Scriptures the things concerning Himself" (Luke 24:27).

The second way God witnessed of His Son was through Christ's works: "Jesus answered them, 'I told you, and you do not believe. The works that I do in My Father's name, they bear witness of Me'" (John 10:25). The miracles Jesus performed were the Father's witness. They revealed that Jesus was who He claimed to be.

The third means of the Father's witness was through direct communication. God actually said in an audible voice, "This is My beloved Son" (Matthew 17:5). The Father, then, is the source of all witness about Christ, as recorded in Scripture: the Old Testament prophecies, the works Jesus did, the words He spoke, and the direct statements of the Father. Your Christian testimony should echo the Father's witness, and that will happen when you study the Word diligently and share it with others.

Witness Is Through the Spirit. "When the Helper comes, whom I shall send to you from the Father, *the Spirit of truth* who proceeds from the Father, He will testify of Me" (John 15:26, emphasis added). Whatever witness God the Father has in the world, He has through the Holy Spirit. The Spirit calls believers into court to testify. He is also "the Spirit of truth," and that reveals the kind of testimony He gives. He cannot be a false witness; He is truth and always declares truth. If Jesus Himself ministered in the power of the Spirit, members of His Body must rely on the Holy Spirit's power to witness.

Today the Holy Spirit dwells within all believing Christians. We carry the witness that proceeds from the Father by the Spirit, and we communicate it to the world. The Holy Spirit has no physical voice; His witnessing is through individual believers. Jesus affirmed that the Spirit "dwells with you, and will be in you" (John 14:17). Acts 4:31 describes witnessing through the Spirit in the early church: "They [believers] were all filled with the Holy Spirit, and they spoke the word of God with boldness."

Christians are qualified to witness not only because of the Holy Spirit within them, but also because they have experienced Jesus Christ firsthand. To witness in a court case, we must have been personally involved in the experience; secondhand testimony is unacceptable.

I will never forget the time I had to testify about a crime I'd witnessed. The court asked me three things: "What did you see?" "What did you hear?" "What did you feel?" I could address those questions because I was an eyewitness. John placed this truth about firsthand experience into the context of the Christian life: "That which was from the beginning, which we have heard, which we have seen with our eyes, which we have looked upon, and our hands have handled, concerning the Word of life . . . we declare to you" (1 John 1:1–3). Our witness is not a detached lecture about Jesus; instead, it declares, "I have seen and heard the Christ, and He has changed my life."

Down through the ages this kind of character witness has been more precious than life itself. The Greek word *martus*, which means "witness," is the source of the term *martyr*, meaning one who dies as a result of his uncompromising stance or testimony. Many times when the early believers stood up as witnesses for Christ, it cost them their lives. The church today needs more who will witness effectively, whatever the cost to their popularity or their lives.

However, it's very important to understand that people are not saved because of your testimony. No one has ever been saved, or ever will be, apart from the working of the Holy Spirit. Although Paul shared the gospel with Lydia, she was not saved until "the Lord opened her heart to heed the things spoken by Paul" (Acts 16:14). Even knowledge of biblical truths will not save anyone apart from the work of the Holy Spirit.

That's a liberating truth. Proclaiming the gospel would be

a terrible burden if a person's salvation depended on our persuasiveness. How comforting to know that we are responsible only to be diligent and faithful in allowing the Holy Spirit to use us.

Witness Is in the Body. If the Holy Spirit indwells every individual member of the church, then logically He indwells the entire body of believers. The apostle Paul said Jesus Christ is "the chief cornerstone, in whom the whole building, being fitted together, grows into a holy temple in the Lord, in whom you also are being built together for a dwelling place of God in the Spirit" (Ephesians 2:20–22). The entire church is the temple of the Holy Spirit, just as the individual member is. The Spirit indwells the corporate Body to witness to the world about the Father and the Son.

The Body presents a single collective testimony in two ways. First, the Body witnesses by its visible unity. Jesus prayed, "I do not pray for these alone, but also for those who will believe in Me through their word; that they all may be one, as You, Father, are in Me, and I in You; that they also may be one in Us, that the world may believe that You sent Me" (John 17:20–21).

The second way the Body witnesses is by love. Jesus told the disciples that love is the mark of all genuine believers: "Little children, I shall be with you a little while longer. You will seek Me; and as I said to the Jews, 'Where I am going, you cannot come,' so now I say to you. A new commandment I give to you, that you love one another; as I have loved you, that you also love one another. By this all will know that you are My disciples, if you have love for one another" (John 13:33–35). The more consistently Christians show love for one another, the more powerful our impact on the world will be. Individual members of the Body are the last link in the witness of the Father. The testimony of Christ must not break down with us. Each Christian must do his part to witness. As we saw at the beginning of this chapter, according to the Bible, witnessing is not an option. Passages such as Matthew 28:19–20 and Acts 1:8 make it clear that we all are responsible to be witnesses for Christ.

You don't have to be well versed in all the intricacies of theology to be an effective witness. The blind man healed by Jesus didn't know how to answer all the theological questions the Pharisees asked, but he could say, "One thing I know: that though I was blind, now I see" (John 9:25). He was able to explain what Jesus had done for him. That's something all Christians can do, regardless of how much or how little theology and apologetics they know.

Even so, continue to study and grow in your faith and your knowledge of theological truths. I hope to encourage you as Paul encouraged Timothy: "Be diligent to present yourself approved to God, a worker who does not need to be ashamed, rightly dividing the word of truth" (2 Timothy 2:15). However you can, whenever you can, be a witness for Christ. It's your privilege to share the greatest news the world has ever known.

10

FIRE ON THE PATHWAY

The pathway of Christianity seems smooth and beautiful when everything in your life is going well. But the power of Christianity becomes most apparent in times of hardship and disappointment. Like a mountain climber who doesn't know how strong his safety rope is until he falls, a Christian doesn't know how genuine his faith is until it is tested. How you respond to a fire on the pathway of life reveals whether your faith is genuine or not.

Everyone endures some measure of trouble. That is the consequence of the Fall, the natural result of sinful human nature and of a world and society corrupted by iniquity. Job 5:7 says, "Man is born to trouble, as the sparks fly upward."

Jesus warned the disciples, "In the world you will have tribulation" (John 16:33). Even as a child of God, you are not exempt from problems. Trouble is inevitable in marriage and family life (1 Corinthians 7:28). You also can expect occasional crises in your job, school, and even in the church. And you can depend on encountering trouble because of your faith. Paul reminded Timothy, "All who desire to live godly in Christ Jesus will suffer persecution" (2 Timothy 3:12). If you are a true believer, affliction will force you to think more deeply about your true spiritual condition, which will free you from self-deception about your salvation and a dependence on self-righteousness.

THE ULTIMATE QUESTION: WHY?

Why should Christians have to suffer? If a merciful and omnipotent God is in control of your life, how can He let horrible things happen? This is probably the most asked question of the past two thousand years! Scripture has the answers to all the questions of life, including that one. When you are burdened by trials, God's Word will comfort you with an understanding of why you need to endure them:

To Test the Strength of Your Faith. God assists us in taking a spiritual inventory of the quality and genuineness of our faith. Those who become bitter and self-pitying when trouble comes clearly expose their weak faith. But those who turn to the Lord as trouble increases demonstrate strong faith.

According to Proverbs 17:3, "The LORD tests the hearts." The apostle Peter said, "In this you greatly rejoice, though now for a little while, if need be, you have been grieved by various trials, that the genuineness of your faith, being much more precious than gold that perishes, though it is tested by fire, may be found to praise, honor, and glory at the revelation of Jesus Christ" (1 Peter 1:6–7).

These tests are not for God's sake, because He already knows what's in your heart. They are for your benefit so you can know if your faith is real or not. But be assured of this: no trial, no matter how severe, can destroy genuine saving faith, because one who is saved "endures to the end" (Matthew 24:13).

To Humble You. Trials remind us to not let our trust in the Lord turn into presumption and spiritual self-satisfaction. The greater our blessings, the more Satan will tempt us to look on them as our own accomplishments or what is rightfully due us, rather than as what we have received entirely from the Lord. Satan wants you to be proud; God wants you to be humble. The apostle Paul recognized, "Lest I should be exalted above measure by the abundance of the revelations, a thorn in the flesh was given to me, a messenger of Satan to buffet me, lest I be exalted above measure" (2 Corinthians 12:7).

To Wean You from Worldly Advantage. The more we accumulate material possessions and worldly knowledge, experience, and notoriety, the more we are tempted to rely on them instead of the Lord. Certain worldly benefits, such as education, success on the job, and honors bestowed are not bad things in themselves, but they can easily become the focus of our concern and the basis of our trust.

One great example of how to treat worldly advantage is Moses: "By faith Moses, when he became of age, refused to be called the son of Pharaoh's daughter, choosing rather to suffer affliction with the people of God than to enjoy the passing pleasures of sin, esteeming the reproach of Christ greater riches than the treasures in Egypt; for he looked to the reward" (Hebrews 11:24–26).

To Call You to an Eternal Hope. The harder our trials become and the longer they last, the more we look forward to being with the Lord. Paul said, "We also glory in tribulations, knowing that tribulation produces perseverance; and perseverance, character; and character, hope. Now hope does not disappoint" (Romans 5:3–5). If your hope is in heaven, you'll never be disappointed by anything in this life. Suffering is the first step in producing that hope.

Paul expressed his heavenly hope when he said, "For our light affliction, which is but for a moment, is working for us a far more exceeding and eternal weight of glory, while we do not look at the things which are seen, but at the things which are not seen. For the things which are seen are temporary, but the things which are not seen are eternal" (2 Corinthians 4:17–18). The greater your trials, the sweeter your hope of heaven becomes.

To Reveal What You Really Love. The great patriarch Abraham's willingness to sacrifice his son Isaac (Genesis 22:1–14; Hebrews 11:17–19) not only proved his faith, but also his supreme love for the Lord. All of God's promises and Abraham's hopes were bound up in Isaac. Yet when God commanded him to kill Isaac as a sacrifice, Abraham was ready to obey. God stopped him, spared Isaac, and provided another sacrifice. But his willingness proved that he loved God above all else, even more than his own son. To love God is the greatest commandment, and here we see that trials help us to love Him as we ought.

To Teach You Obedience. The psalmist acknowledged, "Before I was afflicted I went astray, but now I keep Your word . . . It is good for me that I have been afflicted, that I may learn Your statutes" (Psalm 119:67, 71). The painful sting of affliction ought to remind you that sin has consequences. So God uses trials to make you obey and pursue holiness.

To Teach You to Value God's Blessings. Our reason tells us to value the world and the things of the world, and our senses tell us to value pleasure and ease. But through trials, faith tells us to value the things of God, with which He has blessed us abundantly—including His Word, His care, His provision, His strength, and, of course, His salvation. David declared, "Because Your lovingkindness is better than life, my lips shall praise You. Thus I will bless You while I live; I will lift up my hands in Your name" (Psalm 63:3–4).

To Strengthen You for Greater Usefulness. The more you are tested and refined by trials, the more effective you'll be in serving the Lord. Paul said, "Therefore I take pleasure in infirmities, in reproaches, in needs, in persecutions, in distresses, for Christ's sake. For when I am weak, then I am strong" (2 Corinthians 12:10). Hebrews 11 exalts those godly men and women "who through faith subdued kingdoms, worked righteousness, obtained promises, stopped the mouths of lions, quenched the violence of fire, escaped the edge of the sword, out of weakness were made strong" (verses 33–34).

To Enable You to Help Others in Their Trials. Jesus told Peter, "Simon, Simon! Indeed, Satan has asked for you, that he may sift you as wheat. But I have prayed for you, that your faith should not fail; and when you have returned to Me, strengthen your brethren" (Luke 22:31–32). God allowed Peter to suffer not only to strengthen him for greater usefulness, but also to prepare him to strengthen others. God will use trials to do the same in your life. And we can look to Christ as our example: "For in that He Himself has suffered, being tempted, He is able to aid those who are tempted" (Hebrews 2:18).

RIGHT RESPONSES

Now you know why God brings trials into your life. But what should you do about it? What is your right response? In the same way Scripture explains why trials make you a better Christian, it also tells you how to react. James 1:2–12 details five key responses that will help you to persevere through your trials.

A Joyful Attitude. As a Christian, God has commanded you to view your trials with all joy: "Count it all joy when you fall into various trials" (James 1:2). James is referring to a unique fullness of joy the Lord graciously provides for you when you willingly, and without complaint, endure troubles while trusting Him. You can trust in the promise and goodness of our Lord—that's how you can view trials as a welcome friend.

We are not just to act joyful—we are to be genuinely

joyful. Your joy is to be a matter of your will, not your feelings. It requires a conscious, determined commitment on your part. Since God commands it, you can be sure it is within your ability and under the Spirit's provision. Genuine faith in Christ will result in thanksgiving and rejoicing even in the midst of the worst of troubles.

The more you rejoice in your trials, the more you will realize that they are not liabilities, but privileges, ultimately beneficial and not harmful, no matter how painful they might be at the moment. When you face trials with a joyful attitude, you will discover that the greatest benefit is drawing closer to God, the source of your joy. Trials will force you to seek Him in prayer and to study His Word, which will increase your joy all the more as you experience His presence, goodness, love, and grace.

An Understanding Mind. As you grow in your Christian walk, you will learn from experience as well as your study of God's Word "that the testing of your faith produces patience" (James 1:3). A better translation for *patience* is "patient endurance." Patiently enduring trials while trusting in the Lord develops perseverance, and that has a lasting quality. Once you have experienced and endured affliction or testing, you will discover that your trust in the Lord not only remains, but also is all the stronger because of the testing.

Paul assured all believers that "no temptation has overtaken you except such as is common to man; but God is faithful, who will not allow you to be tempted beyond what you are able, but with the temptation will also make the way of escape, that you may be able to bear it" (1 Corinthians 10:13). The Lord will not allow any of His children to face any temptation that they cannot, in His power and provision, survive. Thus you can know for sure that you will never be called on to face any trial that the Lord has not prepared you to endure.

Paul gladly and without shame endured great suffering because, he said, "I know whom I have believed and am persuaded that He is able to keep what I have committed to Him until that day" (2 Timothy 1:12).

A Submissive Will. God promises no free passes in the Christian life, only that He will see His people through the trials without their suffering spiritual harm. But God will not be able to use those trials to accomplish what they need without our willing submissiveness. When you learn to rejoice in your trials and come to understand that your gracious heavenly Father uses them not to harm but to strengthen and perfect you, that's when you can embrace them as beneficial.

James 1:4 says, "Let patience have its perfect work, that you may be perfect and complete, lacking nothing." "Perfect" is better rendered "mature," referring to spiritual maturity fulfilled in Christlikeness, which is the goal of endurance and perseverance. Paul beautifully expressed the concept of spiritual maturity when he described the Galatians as "my little children, for whom I labor in birth again until Christ is formed in you" (Galatians 4:19).

"Complete" in James 1:4 carries the idea of being whole or entire. And when James added, "lacking nothing," he emphasized that the result of trials is maturity and completeness, which do not lack any spiritual importance and value. Peter tells us the result of our willingness to submit under trials: "May the God of all grace, who called us to His eternal glory by Christ Jesus, after you have suffered a while, perfect, establish, strengthen, and settle you" (1 Peter 5:10).

A Believing and Wise Heart. James 1:5 says, "If any of you lacks wisdom, let him ask of God, who gives to all liberally and without reproach, and it will be given to him." When you are going through any trial, you need a special measure of understanding to help you endure it. That should drive you to your knees to ask God to supply the wisdom you need. Strong, sound faith is not based on feelings but on knowledge and understanding of the promises of God's truth, which is spiritual wisdom.

When you face any kind of trial—physical, emotional,

moral, or spiritual—you need God's wisdom to help you endure. Consider these words of Solomon: "Trust in the LORD with all your heart, and lean not on your own understanding; in all your ways acknowledge Him, and He shall direct your paths. Do not be wise in your own eyes; fear the LORD and depart from evil" (Proverbs 3:5–7). God, and God alone, is the source of wisdom.

Calling on the Lord for wisdom is not an option; it is a command: "let him ask" in James 1:5 is an imperative. If you are not driven to the Lord and do not develop a deeper prayer life as a result of a trial, the Lord is likely to keep you under the test and may even intensify it until you seek Him in prayer. For it is when you approach His throne of grace that you "may obtain mercy and find grace to help in time of need" (Hebrews 4:16).

A Humble Spirit. James 1:9–11 says, "Let the lowly brother glory in his exaltation, but the rich in his humiliation, because as a flower of the field he will pass away. For no sooner has the sun risen with a burning heat than it withers the grass; its flower falls, and its beautiful appearance perishes. So the rich man also will fade away in his pursuits." When God, in His wisdom and sovereignty, takes away physical possessions from some of His children, you can be sure it is for the purpose of making them spiritually mature, a blessing infinitely more valuable than anything they have lost. If God deprives you of something in this life, you can be sure it is temporary and insignificant when compared to your future divine inheritance.

The loss of material things is meant to drive us to the Lord and to greater spiritual maturity, blessing, and satisfaction. At that point, both rich and poor believers are alike. Neither material possessions, nor the lack of them, make any difference to your spiritual walk. What is important is a trusting relationship with the Lord, who showers all of His children with spiritual wealth that will never diminish or fail to satisfy.

YOUR REWARD

James ended his discussion of trials with this statement about the reward of persevering: "Blessed is the man who endures temptation; for when he has been approved, he will receive the crown of life which the Lord has promised to those who love Him" (James 1:12). Perseverance results in God's approval, and His approval brings about the "crown of life." The term for "crown" comes from athletic competition. In James's day a champion received a wreath, which was a symbol of perseverance necessary to win the prize. A more literal translation is "the crown which is life"—in this case, eternal life. So perseverance affirms God's approval because it is evidence of eternal life.

Your perseverance as a Christian in the face of trials and disappointments doesn't produce salvation and eternal life; it is the result and evidence of salvation and eternal life. The fact that you hold fast to the faith—no matter what—is proof you are one of God's own people.

There's a great early American hymn "How Firm a Foundation," that imagines the Lord speaking to Christians and saying:

> When through fiery trials thy pathway shall lie,
> My grace, all sufficient, shall be thy supply;
> The flame shall not hurt thee; I only design
> Thy dross to consume and thy gold to refine.

Dross is the useless waste removed by the refining process, leaving only pure gold behind. The fires of disappointment, despair, and trouble may be frightening at first, but they are signs of the work God is doing in your life, burning away the impurities of your spirit, preparing it for a joyous eternity in heaven.

11

THE JOY OF
A LIVING HOPE

*I*f the hope of this world is all we have to live for, we're in big trouble. The passing world is full of pitfalls and sorrows. I cannot begin to imagine what life in the flesh would be like without the hope of a glorious future beyond this earthly realm. You and I and everyone else who trusts in Jesus Christ for salvation from sin have reason to hope. Our hope is in "new heavens and a new earth in which righteousness dwells" (2 Peter 3:13). We have a heavenly Father who will never desert us, never deceive us, and always love us. Like Abraham, we look for a city "whose architect and builder is God" (Hebrews 11:10 NASB).

All hope apart from Jesus Christ is a dead hope because it is based on a lie. Thus the hopes and dreams of unsaved people die with them. Paul said, "If in this life only we have hope in Christ, we are of all men the most pitiable" (1 Corinthians 15:19). If we put our trust in a savior who can't promise us an eternal future with God, full of righteousness, then we deserve pity.

But what Scripture teaches is not some worldly pipe dream; it is a pervasive reality. Biblical hope is a fact that God has promised and will fulfill. This hope causes us to look to the future with joy and motivates us to pursue Christlikeness here on earth with maximum effort. Hope is central to a life of faith.

THE BASIS OF HOPE

The author of Hebrews said, "This hope we have as an anchor of the soul, both sure and steadfast, and which enters the Presence behind the veil, where the forerunner has entered for us, even Jesus" (6:19–20). Our hope as Christians is solid and unshakable, embodied in Christ Himself, who has entered into God's presence in the heavenly Holy of Holies on our behalf (4:14–16). He serves as our great High Priest, forever interceding before God for us (7:25).

In his first epistle, the apostle Peter offered further proof of the security of our hope: "Blessed be the God and Father of our Lord Jesus Christ, who according to His abundant mercy has begotten us again to a living hope through the resurrection of Jesus Christ from the dead" (1:3). Our hope is based on the resurrection of Christ. On the contrary, "if Christ is not risen, your faith is futile; you are still in your sins!" (1 Corinthians 15:17). The Resurrection is the crown of Christ's atoning work. By His death and resurrection He bore our sins, satisfied the righteousness of God, conquered death, and guaranteed us a living hope in the next life. Those riches are ours through a spiritual rebirth in Him.

All three aspects of our salvation—past, present, and future—are bound up in the gospel. In Titus 1:1–2 Paul wrote "Paul, a bondservant of God and an apostle of Jesus Christ, according to the faith of God's elect and the acknowledgment of the truth which accords with godliness, in hope of eternal life." Paul preached the gospel so that the elect could believe and be saved. That's the past aspect—our justification. Those whom God chooses hear the gospel, believe, and therefore are justified by Him. The present aspect of the gospel is "the acknowledgment of the truth which accords with godliness." That's our sanctification. The future aspect is the "hope of eternal life," which is our glorification.

Romans 8 is a great chapter of promise for us. Here Paul stated that God will fulfill the believer's hope and bring him to glory: "We ourselves groan within ourselves, eagerly waiting for the adoption, the redemption of our body. For we were saved in this hope, but hope that is seen is not hope; for why does one still hope for what he sees? But if we hope for what we do not see, we eagerly wait for it with perseverance" (verses 23–25).

Our hope is glory. We want to experience the redemption of our bodies and finally be rid of the sinful battle in our flesh. That glorious reality of our salvation we have yet to realize. The joys of salvation here and now cannot begin to compare with what God has prepared for us in the future. When our hope is finally fulfilled, we will understand that the greatest elements of our salvation went unrealized in this life.

Even though our hope is in the future, it is guaranteed now. For us, future glory is a present fact. That's why we will persevere while we wait eagerly for our glorification. No matter what trials and struggles we encounter while we wait, we can be sure God will fulfill His calling of us and bring us to glory. Since God made the effort to justify us, we can be sure He will also glorify us.

OUR HOPE

The Bible breaks down the concept of our hope into several components. Here are eleven features of true hope that should produce joy in every Christian heart:

Our Hope Comes from God. Our hope is objective, not subjective. Psalm 43:5 asks, "Why are you cast down, O my soul? And why are you disquieted within me? Hope in God; for I shall yet praise Him, the help of my countenance and my God." There is no reason to despair when God is the source of our hope.

Our Hope Is a Gift of Grace. In 2 Thessalonians 2:16–17, Paul wrote, "Now may our Lord Jesus Christ Himself, and our God and Father, who has loved us and given us everlasting consolation and good hope by grace, comfort your hearts and establish you in every good word and work." The eternal comfort and good hope God gives is not something we deserve; it is a gift of His grace. God gives it to whom He will, according to His own sovereign desires.

Our Hope Is Defined by Scripture. Romans 15:4 says, "Whatever things were written before were written for our learning, that we through the patience and comfort of the Scriptures might have hope." When you need comfort and encouragement, look to God's Word because it will give you hope in the midst of all your trials.

Our Hope Is Reasonable. The apostle Peter said, "Sanctify the Lord God in your hearts, and always be ready to give a defense to everyone who asks you a reason for the hope that is in you, with meekness and fear" (1 Peter 3:15). Our hope is reasonable because it is objectively defined in the Bible. If someone asks you what you think is going to happen to the world in the future, you can explain God's plan from the Scripture.

Our Hope Is Secured by Christ's Resurrection. Peter stated clearly that God "has begotten us again to a living hope through the resurrection of Jesus Christ from the dead" (1 Peter 1:3). Jesus Christ came back from death. More than five hundred people saw Him on one occasion (1 Corinthians 15:6). His own disciples touched Him, talked with Him, and even ate with Him after His resurrection (Luke 24:36–43; John 20:19–21:23). They saw the scars in His hands from His crucifixion. Before He was crucified, Jesus said, "Because I live, you will live also" (John 14:19). That is our hope. Christ went through death and came out the other side alive, opening the way for us.

Our Hope Is Confirmed by the Holy Spirit. Romans 15:13 says, "Now may the God of hope fill you with all joy and peace in believing, that you may abound in hope by the power of the Holy Spirit." The Bible explains your hope, and when you go through some crisis, the Holy Spirit empowers you to endure. Your knowledge of Scripture works in concert with the energizing power of the Spirit to sustain you in your darkest hour, enabling you to hold on to your hope.

Our Hope Is a Defense Against Satan's Attacks. Satan wants you to doubt and question God about the reality of your salvation. But there is a piece of spiritual armor God has provided that will protect you from Satan's attacks. Paul pictures that armor as a helmet, the hope of salvation (1 Thessalonians 5:8). You can remain secure in your salvation because you have knowledge of God's promises throughout Scripture of your eternal redemption (John 6:37–39; 10:28–29; Romans 5:10; 8:31–39; Philippians 1:6; 1 Peter 1:3–5). The Word of God gives you the foundation on which you must build your hope.

Our Hope Is Strengthened Through Trials. On the heels of his instruction about the helmet of salvation, Paul wrote, "For God did not appoint us to wrath, but to obtain salvation through our Lord Jesus Christ, who died for us, that whether we wake or sleep, we should live together with Him. Therefore, comfort each other and edify one another, just as you also are doing" (1 Thessalonians 5:9–11). When you are being drubbed by Satan's attack, or any other trial, that's when you need most of all to turn to God's Word to be reminded that He appointed you to your salvation. And as you build up others with that truth, God will make you even stronger through the trial.

Our Hope Produces Joy. Even in the midst of sorrow, our hope will produce joy. Psalm 146:5 connects these two seemingly opposite emotions: "Happy is he who has the God of Jacob for his help, whose hope is in the LORD his God." The Lord further says, "Blessed is the man who trusts in the LORD, and whose hope is the LORD" (Jeremiah 17:7). When you have hope in God, you have joy.

Our Hope Removes the Fear of Death. Paul wrote, "'O Death, where is your sting? O Hades, where is your victory?' The sting of death is sin, and the strength of sin is the law. But thanks be to God, who gives us the victory through our Lord Jesus Christ" (1 Corinthians 15:55–57). Death can no longer harm us; it is merely the door that ushers us into the presence of the Lord in heaven.

Our Hope Is Fulfilled in Christ's Return. You might have thought that hope is fulfilled right after we die. But death simply gets our spirits to that point—our bodies have yet to be raised. They await the rapture of the church: "For the Lord Himself will descend from heaven with a shout, with the voice of an archangel, and with the trumpet of God. And the dead in Christ will rise first. Then we who are alive and remain shall be caught up together with them in the clouds to meet the Lord in the air. And thus we shall always be with the Lord" (1 Thessalonians 4:16–17). Those who are dead in Christ—whose spirits are already with the Lord—will be united with their glorified bodies. That's when our hope becomes reality.

The church at Thessalonica was a great church. When Paul wrote to its members, he never reprimanded them; he just instructed and commended them. One of his commendations was this: "We give thanks to God always for you all, making mention of you in our prayers, remembering without ceasing your work of faith, labor of love, and patience of hope . . . [knowing you] wait for His Son from heaven" (1 Thessalonians 1:2–3, 10). Are you in that waiting mode? Are you living as if Jesus could come any moment? Are you walking in such a way that if He did come you would be pleased to have Him examine your life? You and I must live every moment as if He might be here in the next, for He may.

A FATHER'S EVERLASTING LOVE

As a Christian you now have the joy and privilege of beginning your life afresh. Like a clear day after a summer rain, your spirit is clean, renewed, and washed clear of all its old dirt and imperfections. Your heavenly Father has welcomed you with open arms into His family, and will nurture and protect you from now on, no matter what troubles may confront you. You can face the world fearlessly, confident that whatever challenges you encounter, an all-knowing and all-loving God put them there for your ultimate good. The more daunting they seem, the further they will go to make you like Christ.

Becoming a Christian won't end your problems; on the contrary, standing up for Christ may make some problems worse. There will still be disappointments and frustrations and failures in your life. But now you know that behind every one of them is a heavenly Father who is working on your behalf, teaching you, loving you, correcting you, and ripening you for heaven. Whatever you've given up of your old life, or whatever you may sacrifice in the future, is worth the price of eternity with Christ.

God the Father loves you more than any earthly father ever could. As the Creator, He knows you better than any earthly father, down to the darkest recesses of your sinful life, yet He loves you anyway. Not because you deserve it—it's a love that cannot be earned—but because He extends His grace and salvation to you as a member of His family.

Sometimes He may seem far away. But remember that His love is ever guiding His will for your life. Then you will never forget that you are His, and that His love will last forever.

ABOUT THE AUTHOR

$\mathscr{J}$OHN MACARTHUR is pastor-teacher of Grace Community Church in Sun Valley, California, as well as author, conference speaker, president of The Master's College and Seminary, and featured teacher with Grace to You.

In 1969, after graduating with honors from Talbot Theological Seminary, John came to Grace Community Church. The emphasis of his pulpit ministry is the careful study and verse-by-verse exposition of the Bible, with special attention devoted to the historical and grammatical background of each passage. Under John's leadership, Grace Community Church's two morning worship services fill the three-thousand-seat auditorium to capacity. Several thousand members also participate each week in dozens of fellowship groups and training programs, most led by lay leaders and each dedicated to equipping members for ministry on local, national, and international levels.

In 1985, John became president of The Master's College (formerly Los Angeles Baptist College), an accredited, four-year liberal arts Christian college in Santa Clarita, California. In 1986, John founded The Master's Seminary, a graduate school dedicated to training men for full-time pastoral roles and missionary work. John is also president and featured teacher with Grace to You. Founded in 1969, Grace to You is the nonprofit organization responsible for developing, producing, and distributing John's books, audiocassettes, audio CDs, and the *Grace to You, Portraits of Grace,* and *Grace to You Weekend* radio programs. Grace to You's outreach extends beyond the United States with offices throughout the English-speaking world in Australia, Canada, Europe, India, New Zealand, and South Africa. *Gracia a Vosotros,* the Spanish version of the *Grace to You* broadcast, also airs more than 450 times daily, reaching 23 countries, including Mexico, Spain, Argentina, Chile, Peru, Venezuela, and Colombia. In its three-decade history, Grace to You has also distributed more than 13 million audiocassette tapes and more than 140 study guide titles.

Since completing his first best-selling book, *The Gospel According to Jesus,* in 1988, John has written more than six dozen books and, through Grace to You and retail bookstores, distributed millions of copies worldwide. Among the bestsellers are titles such as: *The MacArthur Study Bible, Our*

Sufficiency in Christ, Charismatic Chaos, Rediscovering Expository Preaching, Saved Without a Doubt, Ashamed of the Gospel, The Gospel According to the Apostles, Strength for Today, Reckless Faith, The Freedom and Power of Forgiveness, The Glory of Heaven, The Murder of Jesus, The MacArthur New Testament Commentary series, *What the Bible Says About Parenting,* the award-winning children's book *I Believe in Jesus,* and his newest releases, *Lord, Teach Me to Pray; Safe in the Arms of God;* and *Hard to Believe.* Many of John's books are available on CD-ROM, and dozens of titles have been translated into Chinese, French, German, Italian, Japanese, Korean, Marathi, Polish, Romanian, Russian, Spanish, and many other major languages.

John and his wife, Patricia, live in Southern California and have four children (all married), who have given them thirteen grandchildren.

For more details about John MacArthur and all his Bible-teaching resources, contact:

Grace to You at 800-55-GRACE
or *www.gty.org.*

THE MACARTHUR STUDY BIBLE

From the moment you pick it up, you'll know it is a classic. Winner of "The 1998 Study Bible of the Year Award" and featuring the word-for-word accuracy of The New King James Version, it is perfect for serious Bible study.

Since this Bible comes in a variety of styles, visit your bookstore to find the one that's right for you.

OTHER BOOKS BY JOHN MACARTHUR

Lord, Teach Me to Pray

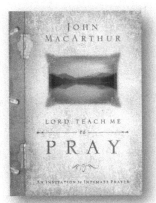

Including examples from John MacArthur's own prayer life, as well as classic Puritan prayers and pages to record personal prayers and God's answers, this beautiful gift book will deepen your fellowship with the Father.
ISBN 1-4041-0024-5

MacArthur LifeWorks Library CD-ROM

The interactivity and ease-of-use *eBible*™ combined with the wealth of material available from John MacArthur provide a powerful electronic library!
ISBN 0-7852-5018-2

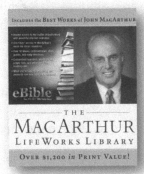

Twelve Ordinary Men

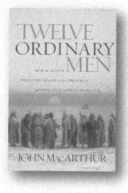

John MacArthur draws principles from Christ's careful, hands-on training of the original twelve disciples (ordinary men—fishermen, tax collectors, political zealots) for today's modern disciple—you.
ISBN 0-8499-1773-5
Cassette ISBN 0-8499-6350-8
Workbook ISBN 0-8499-4407-4

Hard to Believe

In contrast to the superficiality of much modern Bible teaching, John MacArthur uncovers in this book the unvarnished truth of what Christ really taught. In simple, compelling terms, he spells out what is required of those who would follow Him.
ISBN 0-7852-6345-4 • CD ISBN 0-7852-

6152-4
Cassette ISBN 0-7852-6347-0 • Workbook ISBN 0-7852-6346-2

Twelve Extraordinary Women

Join best-selling author and highly esteemed Bible teacher John MacArthur as he studies the lives and faith of key women from both the Old and New Testaments. Written in the same style as his popular book *Twelve Ordinary Men*, each chapter includes a biographical summary of the woman along with spiritual lessons drawn from her life.

ISBN 0-7852-6256-3 • CD ISBN 0-7852-6259-8